Fishing with the Presidents

Fishing with the Presidents

Bill Mares

Tight lines –

Bill Mares

STACKPOLE
BOOKS

Copyright © 1999 by William Mares

Published by
STACKPOLE BOOKS
5067 Ritter Road
Mechanicsburg, PA 17055

Printed in the United States of America

First edition

10 9 8 7 6 5 4 3 2 1

Cover drawing by Jeff Danziger

Library of Congress Cataloging-in-Publication Data

Mares, Bill.
    Fishing with the presidents/Bill Mares. — 1st ed.
        p.   cm.
    Includes bibliographical references (p.   ) and index.
    ISBN 0-8117-0638-9 (paperback)
    1. Fishing—United States—Anecdotes. 2. Presidents—United States—Anecdotes.
    I. Title.
    IN PROCESS
    799.1—dc21

                                                    98-21776
                                                        CIP

DEDICATION:

To Dwight Dickinson, Syl Stempel, and Jake Wheeler, great friends and great anglers, who taught me that fishing is much more than catching fish.

CONTENTS

ACKNOWLEDGMENTS

I would like to thank the following people for their invaluable help. First, and always, my wife Chris Hadsel and secondly, my agent Joan Raines, who believed even when I doubted. Also, Judith Schnell and Jon Rounds, my editors at Stackpole Books. Then, Farrow Allen, Bob Behnke, Dennis Bilger, Cynthia Bittinger, Bob Boilard, Paul Boller, Don Bowden, Katherine Brasco, John Burke, George Bush, Jennifer Capps, Rosalynn Carter, Lucy Caswell, Nancy Crane, Wallace Dailey, Jeff Danziger, Don Daughenbaugh, Wally Eagle, Don Ebright, John Engels, Mary Finch, Gerald Ford, Brent Frazee, Debbie Goodsite, Jill Grisco, Fred Hadsel, Wayne Harpster, George Harvey, Mark Hatfield, Tom Hennessey, William Humphrey, Brooks Jackson, Bill Jenney, Don and Alana Johnson, John Kifner, Howard Kirschenbaum, Christopher Koss, Paul Lancaster, Bud Leavitt, David Lendt, Dianne Lynch, Mark Mastromarino, Jon Mathewson, Tom Matthews, Dale Mayer, Bob McGown, Barbara McMillan, Arthur Milnes, Sylvia Naguib, Barbara Natanson, Scott Nollen, Herb Pankratz, Rhey Plumbley, Susan Popkin, Mark Renovitch, John Rhodehamel, Pamela Bates Richards, Mrs. James Roosevelt, Tweed Roosevelt, Paul Schullery, Nancy Snedeker, Russ Soli, David Stanhope, Stephen Stappenbeck, Hazel Stitt, Ralph Swenson, Gary Tanner, Raymond Teichman, Pauline Testerman, Phoebe Tritton, Gil Troy, Dorothy Twohig, Linda Verigan, Jim Welch, Stan Widman.

Of the institutions I am indebted to, first and foremost is the American Museum of Fly-Fishing in Manchester, Vermont. There, with its then-director Don Johnson, I launched this five-year project. Other help came from: George W. Bush Library; Jimmy Carter Library; Coolidge Foundation; Dwight D. Eisenhower Library; Gerald Ford Library; President Warren G. Harding Home; Benjamin Harrison Home; Rutherford B. Hayes Center; Herbert Hoover Library; John F. Kennedy Library; Lincoln Home National Historic Site; Richard Nixon Library; Franklin D. Roosevelt Library; Harry S Truman Library; Washington Papers at the University of Virginia; Alderman Library, University of Virginia; National Archives; Library of Congress; Mount Vernon Ladies Association; Bailey-Howe

Library, University of Vermont; Douglas County Historical Society, Wisconsin; Houghton Library, Harvard University; The Antique Boat Museum, Clayton, New York; Montana Historical Society; Ohio Historical Society; Wyoming Historical Society; Vermont Historical Society; New Hampshire Historical Society; Massachusetts Historical Society; University of Texas—Newspaper Project; University of Iowa Library; Corbis Bettmann Archives; Associated Press; Cartoon Research Center at Ohio University; Fletcher Free Library, Burlington, Vermont; Brooklyn Public Library; *Louisville Courier-Journal; Milwaukee Journal-Sentinel; New York Times; Kansas City Star; Evansville (Ind.) Courier; Burlington (Vt.) Free Press; Washington Post; Washington Star; Deh Cho Drum,* Ft. Simpson, NWT; *Camden Courier-Post; Cleveland Plain-Dealer.*

FOREWORD

Most of our presidents, even those on the dull side, rejected the all-work-and-no-play principle. They took time off from pressing duties to relax, forget the cares of office, and renew their spirits. John Quincy Adams took daily swims in the Potomac, Abraham Lincoln enjoyed leisurely walks in the nation's capital, William Howard Taft found plenty of time to play golf, and Theodore Roosevelt managed to combine what he called "the strenuous life"—hiking, swimming, tennis, boxing, and horseback riding—with a conscientious performance of his presidential responsibilities. James K. Polk, it is true, was such a workaholic that he found no time for play, but he was an exception. Even Calvin Coolidge, whose natural inclination was toward lethargy, finally took up fishing under the prodding of Secret Service chief Edmund Starling and came to love the sport.

In learning how to fish, Coolidge was embracing one of the favorite sports of America's chief executives. Just about all the presidents dabbled in the piscatorial art, at least occasionally, and some of them became expert fishermen. Herbert Hoover, who wrote lovingly about fishing, called it the "silent sport." It provided, he said, "one of the few opportunities given a president for the refreshment of his soul and the clarification of his thoughts by solitude." It provided an escape from the workaday world, too, he noted, especially from the press. Grover Cleveland, another master fisherman, sought relief "from the wearing labor and perplexities of official duty" in his fishing excursions, and he exulted in "the mental and physical restoration" he derived from the sport.

George Bush felt as Cleveland did. Fishing, he declared, "totally, totally clears your mind. . . . It's not just catching the fish; it's the background, the environment, the beauty of it all. You can get just mesmerized by the waves and the clear surf. So I get a kick out of not just catching or trying to catch a fish, but from being in this setting." Franklin D. Roosevelt liked fishing because it gave him an opportunity to escape Washington and "get a perspective" on things that he couldn't get in the White House. "You have to go a long ways off," he said, "so as to see things in their true perspective." Unlike Cleveland and Hoover, FDR also enjoyed the sociability that went with his own fishing expeditions. Sometimes he fished—and chatted—with Winston Churchill. Other times he had a gaggle of presidential aides with him when he went fishing. Like FDR, Dwight D. Eisenhower liked having fishing companions with him on occasion. Jimmy Carter also took fishing buddies (including his wife) with him from time to time when he went off to fish.

In his survey of presidential fishing, William Mares has put together a treasure trove of stories, quotations, pictures, sketches, and cartoons of the presidents who followed in the footsteps of the celebrated Isaac Walton. He places special emphasis on the presidents for whom fishing was a major activity—Washington, Cleveland, Hoover, FDR, Eisenhower, Carter, and Bush—but he also has something to say about the presidents for whom fishing was only a minor sport. He explains the reasons for the passion for fishing among our presidents and examines the reactions of the American public toward the "Fishermen-Presidents." He finds much humor in the subject, but he is serious about it, too. After all, he is a devoted fisherman himself and knows whereof he speaks. He has written an engaging and enlightening study of presidential fishing that even nonfishers can enjoy.

Paul F. Boller Jr.
Author, *Presidential Anecdotes, Presidential Campaigns*
and *Presidential Wives*
August 1997

INTRODUCTION
"ALL MEN ARE EQUAL BEFORE FISH"

In these sad and ominous days of mad fortune-chasing, every patriotic, thoughtful citizen, whether he fishes or not, should lament that we have not among our countrymen more fishermen. —Grover Cleveland

Fishing is great discipline in the equality of men—because all men are equal before fish! —Herbert Hoover

As President, I was able to save with the stroke of the pen a hundred million acres of wilderness area in Alaska. This is the kind of thing that is gratifying to a President, but to be on a solitary stream with good friends, with a fly rod in your hand, and to have a successful or even an unsuccessful day—they're all successful—is an even greater delight. —Jimmy Carter

I like to fish because it is totally relaxing. I love the water. I can concentrate and forget all my worries. I count my blessings while fishing.
—George Bush

It was the last day of the 1990 Vermont Legislature—or at least I hoped so. Historically, these sessions of our citizen body ran from January through April, but they had begun to stretch into May by the time I was elected in the 1980s. With no fixed date of adjournment, no fifteenth round or ninth inning, the end came only after the leadership grew exhausted.

This was my last term. Six years was enough. Citizen legislatures ought to turn over. Even this one in tiny Vermont was being transformed into an ever more professional, longer-lasting, grueling job. Besides, as April stretched into May my thoughts turned to fishing. Every time I drove down to or left the capital of Montpelier, my thoughts turned to fishing, for the Winooski River meanders through the capital two hundred meters from the statehouse, beckoning anglers of all ages and skills. Since the beginning of fishing season, I had kept my gear in the car, just in case I had a free moment.

On this evening I had nothing to do but wait. At about six o'clock the Speaker gave us an hour and a half break for dinner. Having seen deadlines slip before, I knew that that meant at least two hours. I didn't need dinner—I had a candy bar in the car. I grabbed my rod, my waders, and my vest, and I shot down to the river.

It was a fine evening, as the English would say, meaning that a fine rain was falling. Through the mist, I could see fish rising in the pool beneath the railroad bridge behind the gray Transportation Agency building. As I donned my waders, I could see fish rising beneath the trestle. Sliding down the wet-granite blocks of embankment, I entered the water and moved slowly toward the center of the river. Upstream, the biggest rises were on the far side and unreachable, but there were some smaller dimples in the slick ahead.

With shaking fingers I tied on a #16 Adams, greased its fur with the oil and sweat off my nose, and worked out enough line to reach the nearest fish. There was no wind and no sound except the lapping of the current around my knees. With no one around, I was suspended in space. Holding my breath, I made two or three false casts and then tried to lay the fly down above the nearest riser. My first cast fell short. The second one went too far. Damn! But these were tolerant, or hungry, fish. They kept rising.

A mote of gold appeared in my left eye. Over the top of the bank, I could see the ghostly dome of the statehouse rising out of the mist. In twenty minutes I had utterly forgotten the life-and-death issues of criminal sentencing, family court, upland-streams protection, highway-fund diversions, school portfolios, and a host of other worthy matters. Here, I answered to no constituent but myself. . . .

Suddenly the rod bent, and a twelve-inch rainbow lit up the dark-gray water. Then it was gone, thief of my inattention. I cast again. And again. Then I hooked one for keeps. Back and forth, the small brown crisscrossed the slick until I netted it, admired its yellow hue, and released it downstream. Then another rainbow, another brown. In an hour, I caught six fish and released them all. None was over eleven inches, but when I clambered out of the river and back to the statehouse, no sponsor of a new law was happier than I.

The next year I left politics to teach history. "Probably less adolescent behavior in high school than in Montpelier!" remarked one of my new colleagues. My fondness for fishing, however, didn't slacken. At every opportunity I fished the rivers of the state from Canaan in the northeast to Bennington in the south. It was on a trip to the Battenkill one June day that I decided to drop by the American Museum of Fly-Fishing in Manchester.

The museum had been founded in a spare room at the Orvis Company store, but over the years it established an independent presence and grew to have a $400,000 annual budget. The museum's director, Don Johnson, was a big, friendly fellow who loved Hemingway and hockey as well as fishing and who had an encyclopedic knowledge of such minutiae as the nicknames of British Army regiments. He turned me loose to wander through the exhibits of reels, rods, fishing gear, prints, and paintings of salmon and trout fishing.

As with most museums, the bulk of the collection was stored away—over 1,500 rods and reels and a library of some 3,000 books. Among them were not just the classic texts of such anglers as Robert Barnwell Roosevelt, Roderick Haig-Brown, Arnold Gingrich, Ernest Schwiebert, and Lee Wulff but many other articles, volumes, and artifacts as well. Jon Mathewson, the museum curator, also pointed out John Quincy Adams's fly wallet with flies from the 1830s, a fly box from Herbert Hoover, and fly rods donated by both George Bush and Jimmy Carter. Other presidential material included Carter's *An Outdoor Journal*, which I knew about, that recounted both his fishing philosophy and enough details about his joy-filled excursions around the globe to keep any fisherman entertained and envious. Two other books caught my eye, one by Grover Cleveland and one by Herbert Hoover.

Sitting down at Mathewson's pin-neat desk, I slowly turned the age-stained pages of an autographed copy of Cleveland's *Fishing and Shooting Sketches*. In gothic prose, he described the joys of fishing and in one notable passage defended his chosen recreation against the philistines:

> The narrow and ill-conditioned people who snarlingly count
> all fishermen as belonging to a lazy and good-for-nothing class,
> and who take satisfaction in describing an angler's outfit as a
> contrivance with a hook at one end and a fool at the other,
> have been so thoroughly discredited that no one could wish for
> their more irredeemable submersion.

In his *Fishing for Fun,* Herbert Hoover laid out all the reasons why angling is good for us—"to wash your soul"—and good for society by quoting a 4,000-year-old Assyrian tablet: "The gods do not subtract from men's lives the hours spent fishing."

There were also several articles on presidential fishing implying that many of the chief executives had fished at one time or other. The germ of a book began to form. Impulse became resolve, and within a month I was at the Franklin Delano Roosevelt Library in Hyde Park, New York. There would be dozens of other stops over the next four years.

My fascination with presidential fishing itself became a fishing expedition—nay, scores of fishing expeditions, in their variety, excitement, disappointments, and ultimate catch. The nibbles and strikes were not just how presidents fished or whom they fished with or what they wrote about their experiences. There were gems of writing, like the whimsical correspondence between Grover Cleveland and his friend the actor Joe Jefferson or George Washington's testy letters to suppliers of his fishing equipment or Carter's intervention in a dispute over the labeling of imported flies.

Just as interesting were the ways in which the public, press, and friends responded to presidential fishing. There were dozens of editorial cartoons about presidential fishing per se and hundreds more that used fishing as a metaphor to treat the issues of the day. In various presidential archives were thousands of letters and gifts sent by ordinary citizens to offer advice, fellow feeling, or invitations to fish on a favorite pond or stream.

Presidents, I found, had fished everywhere—in Georgia sloughs, on Pennsylvania streams, Adirondack lakes, Kentucky creeks, Wisconsin, Oregon, Colorado, and Wyoming rivers, off the coasts of Maine, Florida, and Texas, in Alaska and off the Galapagos, down the Potomac and up the Amazon. They had lodged in luxury and tented in simplicity. They had pursued the lordly salmon and the lowly perch. They had caught bluefish and trout, tarpon and bass, pickerel and cod, shad and herring, grouper and perch, catfish and pike.

In many ways, the fishing presidents have encountered the same experiences as the rest of us. They have brought home their limit, and they have been skunked. They have killed fish, and they have released others to fight again. They have told the truth, and they have lied when they could get away with it. They have been torn between competition and contemplation. They fished with cronies and they fished alone, the Secret Service notwithstanding.

Yet presidents also had fishing experiences that were uniquely presidential. Calvin Coolidge had Secret Service agents shoo away anglers who dared to fish waters reserved for him. Dwight Eisenhower failed to catch any of the hatchery trout dumped into a Vermont stream the night before his arrival. And only a former president like Jimmy Carter could compare the theft of two prized fly rods to defeat in a national election.

Fishing has never been a partisan sport—men of both parties enjoyed it. Democrats Cleveland and Carter loved to fly fish, and Republicans Coolidge and Bush were happy with bait. Neither was it elitist—only desperate campaign workers would coin the 1936 slogan: Give me a fishing pole and call me Roosevelt!

At its most elementary, this is a book of anecdotes about the presidents and their fishing, how they began to fish, where they practiced it, and what they said or wrote about it. On a more intellectual level, this book is also a thematic exploration of the relationship between the presidents and the public through the experience of recreational fishing. It examines the president as a cultural icon. In the late twentieth century, Americans are ambivalent about the appropriate demeanor of their presidents. We want presidents as remote as royalty and as close as next-door neighbors. We want soaring speeches, and we are titillated by locker-room expletives. Most of the public cannot imagine setting trillion-dollar budgets or planning wars or log-rolling with Congress, but they can imagine how it feels to hook a striped bass or lose a trout.

This book is about presidential recreation, not statecraft, although the inescapable backdrop of war and peace, boom and bust, promise and deceit, and the aching, lonely responsibility of the office gives many of these fishing stories their luster and life. When presidents themselves equate angling with democracy, as Hoover did—"Fishing is great discipline in the equality of men because all men are equal before fish!"—what better excuse could there be to . . . go fishing?

CHAPTER ONE

THE FIRST
"FIRST ANGLER"

For two months during the sweltering summer of 1787, the Federal Convention met in Philadelphia to draw up a constitution for the United States. The convention adjourned from July 26 until August 6 to allow a detail committee to report back with a draft document for the collective deliberation.

The president of that convention, George Washington, did not have time to go all the way back to Mount Vernon during the break. Instead, as his diary tells us, he went fishing.

July 30, 1787: In company with Mr. Govr. Morris and in his Phaeton with my horses, went up to one, Jane Moore's [in which house we lodged] in the vacinity of Valley Forge to get Trout.

July 31, 1787: Whilst Mr. Morris was fishing, I rid over the [whole] Cantonment of the American [army] of the Winter 1777 and 8; visited all the Works, wch were in Ruins, and the Incampments in woods where the grounds had not been cultivated.

On my Return to Mrs. Moore's I found Mr. Robt. Morris and his lady there. [Spent the day there fishing &ca and lodged at the same place.]

August 3, 1787: In company with Mr. Robt. Morris and his Lady, and Mr. Gouvr. Morris I went up to Trenton on another Fishing party. [Dined and] lodged at Colo. Sam Ogden's at the Trenton Works. In the Evening fished, not very successfully.

August 4, 1787: In the morning, and between breakfast and dinner,
    fished again with more success (for perch) than yesterday.[1]

Two days later, George Washington was back at work, guiding the
convention to its conclusion.

How tantalizing to read those lines! Did the fishing renew his energy
and spirit? What was his equipment like? Did he brag about his catches to
Adams and Madison and Jay? Did he dream of those trout while the delegates debated the Virginia plan? Could he forget the deliberations over a
presidency and the commerce clause when he saw risers? We don't know,
but one likes to think so.

We do know that Washington was no novice fisherman. As early as
1751, when he was nineteen, he made notes in his journal about angling
on a voyage to Barbados:

Oct. 7, 1751: A Dolphin we catchd at Noon but cou'd not intice with a
    baited hook two Baricootas, wich played under our stern for some
    Hours; the Dolphin being small we had it dressed for Supper.[2]

Thereafter, he made a number of irregular references to recreational
angling:

1768–May 30: Went fishing and dined under Mr. L. Washington's
    shore. . . .
1770–September 3: Went in the Evening a fishing with my Brothers
    Saml and Charles.
        September 14: Rid to the Mill and Ditchers in the forenoon
    with my Brother; in the afternoon went a fishing.
        October 25: About half way in the long reach we incampd,
    opposite to the beginning of a large bottom on the East side of the
    River. At this place we through out some Lines at Night and
    found a Cat fish of the size of our largest River Cats hooked to it
    in the morning, tho it was of the smallest kinds here.
1772–August 11: Went with those Gentlemn a Fishing, and Dined
    undr the Bank at Colo. Fairfax's near his White Ho. . . .[3]

George Washington fished for recreation throughout his life.[4] But if
we look at the record of his sport fishing, we wouldn't rank him much
higher than John Quincy Adams or Martin Van Buren.

Fishing.

There are no known drawings of Washington himself fishing, but this print from The Sportman's Dictionary, London, 1735, *gives a flavor of the sport fishing he practiced.*
MOUNT VERNON LADIES ASSOCIATION.

It is as a commercial fisherman that George Washington stands out. Indeed, it is probable that Washington was the only president who made a substantial part of his living from fishing. In 1982, John Rhodehamel, the former archivist of Mount Vernon, wrote a fine summary of Washington's complex and far-flung fishing enterprises.

Of all his commercial activities in Fairfax County, George Washington's Potomac fisheries were the most consistently profitable. The Potomac, he wrote in 1793, "was a River well-stocked with various kinds of fish in all Seasons of the year, and in the Spring with Shad, Herring, Bass, Carp, Perch, Sturgeon, etc., in great abundance. The borders of the [Mount Vernon] estate are washed by more than ten miles of tidewater, the whole shore, in fact, is one entire fishery. Accounts of the fantastic richness of the Potomac in past centuries seem scarcely creditable today. An early explorer reported that he could not thrust his sword into the water without spearing a fish, and an eighteenth-century observer wrote that the entire surface was white with thrashing shad and herring during the spring spawning run. Julian Neimcewicz, who visited Mount Vernon in 1798, told of one hundred thousand herring hauled ashore in a single day. The sober entries in George Washington's meticulous account books confirm these fish stories. In his forty years at Mount Vernon, the harvest from the river usually surpassed the crops Washington labored to bring forth on shore. The corn might parch in the fields and the hessian fly might devastate the wheat, but the fisheries yielded abundantly year after year. One of Washington's own maps of his five farms shows the main fishery on the shore of Union farm a mile or so south of the mansion. Two buildings appear at the site, no doubt used for storing the boats, nets, and other equipment during the slack season, as fishing at Mount Vernon was very much a seasonal activity. When the shad and herring made their run up the river in March, April, and May, the work engaged a good part of Washington's labor force. In preparation, a small fleet of boats was caulked and tightened, great seine nets, some as much as five hundred feet long, were spread along the shore for repair, and mounds of salt were assembled while a crew of coopers made barrels to receive the catch. When the fish appeared, the work became feverish. "I again repeat," Washington admonished his overseer, "that when the Schools of fish run, you must draw day and night." The nets were positioned in the rivers in long arcs, sometimes suspended between two boats, sometimes with one end on shore. As they filled, the slave crew hauled them ashore, dumping great piles of silvery fish to be salted down and packed into barrels. Some of the best hauls were made at night under the light of torches and lanterns as the slaves worked in shifts. The Mount Vernon storehouse account books show that the slave fishermen were rewarded with a pint of rum a day.

In many years, the herring catch was numbered in the millions, the shad in the tens of thousands. Much of each spring's harvest was kept at Mount Vernon, for as Washington wrote, fish made up "the larger part of the flesh diet of my people." The fish were also sold to neighbors, to merchants in Alexandria, and exported to the West Indies. Mount Vernon herring developed an international reputation for quality. Washington wrote that his fish sold for 25 shillings a barrel in Jamaica, while barrels from other Potomac fisheries brought only half that. The reason may have been the close attention the master of Mount Vernon paid to the packing of his catch; a buyer soon learned that there was little chance of rotten fish in casks bearing the Washington brand.

In harvesting the bounty of the river before his home, as in coaxing crops from his land, leading an army, or founding a nation, Washington was a meticulous and, far more than his contemporaries, a successful man.[5]

Reading through Washington's journals, looking at this one small topic of fishing, one sees the same extraordinary attention to detail that Washington brought to war and statecraft.

In a 1772 letter to one supplier he detailed the dimensions and quality of the seines because the ones sent the previous year had had meshes too big and too "strait rig'd. . . . I would not wish to have them made of thick heavy twine as they are more liable to heat and req'r great'r force to Work them; keep this Letter by you and I can from time to time point out any alter'ns I may find necessary to make in the future with greater ease and certainty. I am Gentn, etc."[6]

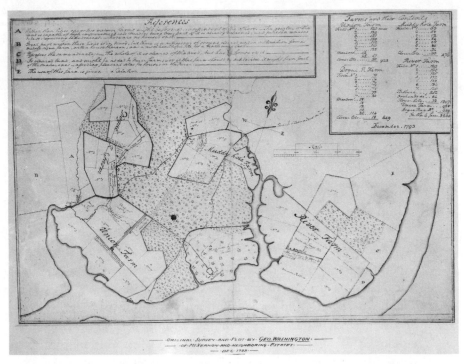

Washington's hand-drawn plot of his Mount Vernon estate in 1793 pinpointed his fishery at Posey's landing on the Union Farm's shore of the Potomac River. Slaves used seines to drag in hundreds of thousands of pounds of shad and herring. THE HUNTINGTON LIBRARY. REPRODUCED BY PERMISSION.

In addition to the constant arguments with suppliers, Washington had to defend his territorial rights. For at least four days in 1760 Washington quarreled with a mysterious "Oyster Man." As he wrote in his journal,

> The Weather continuing Bad & ye same causes subsisting I confind myself to the House. Morris, who went to work yesterday caught cold and was laid up bad again, and several of the Family were taken with the Measles, but no bad Symptoms seemed to attend any of them. Hauled the Sein and got some fish, but was near being disappointd of my Boat by means of an Oyster Man who had lain at my Landing and plagud me a good deal by his disorderly behavior.
>
> Sunday, 6th. The Chariot not returng time enough from Colo. Fairfax's, we were prevented from Church. Mrs. Washington was a good deal better today but the Oyster Man still

continuing his Disorderly behavior at my Landing, [and] I was obligd in the most preemptory manner to order him and his compy away, which he did not incline to obey till next morning.[7]

Salted herring was an important part of a Mount Vernon slave's diet and was distributed at twenty per person per month. Washington cautioned against expecting that the herring "glut" would provide all that the slaves needed. Keep "a sufficiency of fish" from the early runs, he charged his manager.

Washington's letters to his farm managers are full of very detailed instructions, queries, and observations on market and weather conditions.

In one letter he wrote: "As your prospect for grain is discouraging, it may, in a degree, be made up in a good fishing season for herrings; that for shad must, I presume, be almost, if not quite, over."[8]

Washington was well aware that one good season did not assure another: "Unless the weather grows warmer your fishing this season will, I fear, prove unproductive; for it has always been observed that in cold and windy weather the fish keep in deep water and are never caught in numbers, especially at shallow landings."[9]

On the other hand, too many fish could be as vexing as too few:

In the height of the fishery they are not prepared to cure or otherwise dispose of them as fast as they could be caught; of course the seines slacken in their work, or the fish lie and spoil when that is the only time I can make anything by the seine, for small hauls will hardly pay for the wear and tear of the seine and the hire of the hands.[10]

Getting what he considered a fair price was a continual problem for Washington. In 1794 he wrote to his manager:

I am of opinion that selling [the fish] all to one man is best . . . if Mr. Smith will give five shillings per thousand for herring and twelve shillings a hundred for shad and will oblige himself to take all you have to spare, you had better strike and enter into a written agreement with him. . . . If you do not sell to Smith the next best thing is to sell to the watermen. . . . I again repeat that when the schools of fish run you must draw night and day; and whether Smith is prepared to take them or not, they must be caught and charged to him, for it is then and then only I have a return for my expense, and then it is the want of several purchases is felt, for unless one person is extremely well prepared he cannot dispose of the fish as fast as they can be drawn at those times and if seine or seines do no more than keep pace with his convenience my harvest is lost and of course my profit; for the herring will not wait to be caught as they are wanted to be cured.[11]

In one case, Washington had to deal with an agent who, against instructions, sold the contents of his shipment of herring and flour bound for Jamaica. He wrote to a merchant in Jamaica, giving him power of attorney to "settle, Sue for, and recover the proceeds of my Flour, and the price of my Herrings" and to force the agent to "pay into your hands the sums respectively due to me."[12]

During the Revolution, Washington drew on his fishing experience to seek sustenance for his starving troops and wrote about it. There may have been other times as well because food supplies were perennially short, as this letter to Governor George Clinton of New York illustrates:

> Headquarters, New Windsor, April 29, 1781
> Dear Sir: I have received your Excellency's favor of Yesterday with the inclosures, by [C]ol. Nicoll. . . . General Heath informed me yesterday, that there was but one day's allowance of the Irish Beef left in the store, and that not a barrel had arrived at the Garrison from the Eastward. Thus unpromising, your Excellency sees, our prospects of supplies and transportation are!
> I have ordered a quantity of Fish to be contracted for, on this River. And will still persist in using my best endeavors to keep the Army together, and to afford as much protect to the Country, as the means entrusted to me shall enable me to do. I have the honor etc.[13]

Three days later Washington wrote to Brigadier James Clinton:

> Dear Sir: Since my Letter to you, of yesterday, in which I mentioned the measure I had taken respecting supplies, informed you of our only resources, and authorized military coertion in cases of extremity: I have received your favor of the 30th [of April] with a Postscript of the 1st [of May].

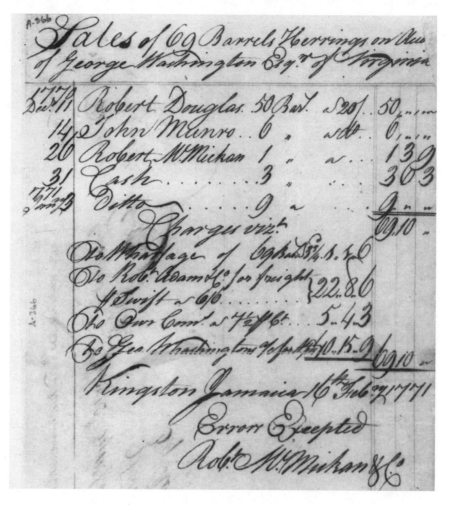

Illustration of Washington's account with a Jamaican firm to whom he delivered sixty-nine barrels of herring in February 1771. MOUNT VERNON LADIES ASSOCIATION.

Alarmed at the critical situation of the Garrison of Fort Schuyler, I ordered out of the small pittance in our Magazines, 50 barrels of Meat and the same quantity of flour, to be transported from this Army, and instantly thrown into that Garrison, but the Commissary reports there are but 34 Bbs of Meat in store. I have directed this number to be sent and the residue of the 50 Bbs to be made up, from the Fish lately barreled on the River. This supply (the Fish included or not, as you think proper) you will be pleased to consider as solely designed for the relief of the

Garrison of Fort Schuyler, and sacredly to be appropriated to that and no other purpose whatever: For in our present embarassed circumstances, when we know not from whence the supplies of tomorrow are to be derived, no inferior object could have justified the Measure of stripping this Army of its last Mouthful. . . .[14]

Despite Washington's obvious concern, the record shows that the troops responded to fish with as much enthusiasm as George Bush would greet broccoli. They held out for beef, which eventually came.

Washington's success and the fisheries' location periodically brought speculators who offered a flat fee for a season's take. However, Washington told his manager that "under all chances fishing yourself will be more profitable than hiring out the landing for 60 pounds."[15]

Despite the regular profits, the burden of the fishery grew heavier and the temptation to turn over the fishery to the speculators increased. By 1787 Washington wrote: "A good rent would induce me to let [the fishery] that I have no trouble or perplexity about it."[16]

Washington's combination of commercial and recreational fishing would never be matched by any other president. In angling, as in so many other areas, Washington was unique.

CHAPTER TWO

ANGLING PRESIDENTS AS ANGLING YOUTHS

Every true fisherman must have an affection for his neighbors, and especially for the barefoot boy whence we all started our fishing careers.

—*Herbert Hoover*

Once when asked what he remembered about the War of 1812 with Great Britain, Abraham Lincoln replied, "Nothing but this: I had been fishing one day and caught a little fish, which I was taking home. I met a soldier on the road, and having been always told at home that we must be good to soldiers, I gave him my fish."

In this brief story we see combined two of the main attractions of fishing: the satisfaction of the catch and the sharing of the result.

Thereafter, Lincoln didn't fish much until he had his own children, and he took them on Sunday outings to fish along the Sangamon River near Springfield, Illinois.[1]

Alas, we don't know much else about his fishing—and so it is with most of the other presidents when it comes to records of their boyhood fishing. It is likely that most of them did fish because most came from rural backgrounds, and that is what most boys from rural backgrounds did. On lazy ponds in Georgia, slow-moving creeks in Kansas, in swift streams in Oregon, off the rocks of Maine, these men/boys likely fished as we all would—for pure joy. But proving it is another matter. Their youthful fishing gave no hint of greatness. None had an angling Boswell to record their triumphs and defeats. Only with the air of retrospect can we inflate these stories to ones of high drama and future promise. Even to achieve this, we must rely upon small and scattered shards of evidence such as the following excerpts that come from the diaries of John Quincy Adams. He was nineteen when he wrote them:

7 May 1787: This morning I went up with Cranch, Learned, Lloyd & Mason, Phelps & Putnam to the fresh pond on fishing and did not return til after four in the afternoon; We caught only a few small fish and had the pleasure of rowing a clumsy boat all over the pond.

What the historian is left with is the imagination—to fill in those gaps between words, to imagine J. Q. Adams's wife, unwilling to stay at home, and heading for the Cohasset or Quincy harbors to fish with their son, Charles Francis, who records in his diary:

7 Oct. 1831: Mornings clear and warm. I passed it in an unsatisfactory way, unless I may consider myself as having provided my father's table with its best dish. I went to fish, and soon after my mother and I. Hull joined us. We had excellent sport catching more than seven dozen of smelt among us. But it took us until dinner time.

9 Oct. 1832: Remained at Home all day and consumed a quantity of it in fishing in company with my Mother. We had very moderate success. Just enough to be tempted to try for more.

16 Oct. 1832: Returned to Quincy, and wasted the afternoon with my mother in fruitless fishing.

15 Sept. 1835: Sandwich Menomet Ponds. Very windy, but J. Q. insisted on going. Mr. T. Hedge and young Russell with myself went with him in the boat to a point about 30 rods from the land. We caught very few and what was worse, I became very seasick. This was doleful. I had no disposition to fish if I had had ever so many bites which I had not. My father caught two cod fish, [which] made him content to return and glad I was when we trod on terra firma again.

17 Sept. 1835: Nantucket. Father went out with I. P. Davis. [They] returned with moderate success . . . my father's arrival had been expected and there was a very large collection of people assembled on the wharf for the purpose of looking at him. This was never pleasant and with him particularly otherwise on account of his entire unfitness for public exhibition.

3 Aug. 1837: Arose very early this morning for the purpose of going by _____with my father to Hingham on a fishing party. My impression was that we were to go down on a sloop but it turned out after reaching Mr. Loring's that we were to go on to Cohasset.

My father accompanied Mr. Loring, and Mr. Quincy Thaxter went with me. We went down to Mr. Nichol's place a mile or two beyond the bank where formerly stopped when here seven years ago. There we were joined by about twenty of the people of Hingham—a portion went out in boats and a part fished from the rocks—I was of the former number and did very well. . . . The day was overcast with a fine breeze from the land. . . . But in the afternoon we had a severe thunder shower after we were housed. . . . The house was a very poor one and the country was desolate enough—the Cohasset rocks form one of the most dangerous points upon the coast in winter time. . . . We had a fish dinner from our sport and were detained sometime by the rain. . . .

Theodore Roosevelt—the pugilist, naturalist, cowboy, Rough Rider, police commissioner, intrepid explorer and hunter of big animals, and evangelist of the "Strenuous Life"—was little known for his fishing. And yet, as Paul Schullery points out in an article in the *American Fly Fisher*, TR did quite a bit of fishing as a youth.[2] In his *Diaries of Boyhood and Youth*, Roosevelt described a vacation by stagecoach to northern New York around Paul Smiths and Lake Osgood (where Calvin Coolidge would spend a summer in 1926). With his father, three guides, brother, and cousin, Theodore went into the woods by boat and a five-mile portage through the woods. Even at the age of twelve, his unquenchable energy was manifest. (His spelling remains in its natural state.)

August 7th/71: Father, Uncle Hill and we three boys [West Roosevelt, a cousin, and Elliott, his brother] went off on an excursion (with our lunch). Of course we went in boats. We passed through the lower St. Regis (on which Paul Smiths is situated), through Spitfire into upper St. Regis. Here we got off the boats upset them (first taking out the lunch) and swam around them. We finally got the boats rightside up again and rowed to an island where we had some revolver practice. . . . In the afternoon we flyfished for trout and caugt—two minnows.

In the bush, August 8th: We finally arrived at a small stream where we were about to launch our boats, when a thunder shower coming up, forced us to turn them upside down and get under then. While in the lake we saw other kinds of wild ducks, loons and a great blue heron. While going down the stream we saw numerous tracks of deer and occasionally of wolves and bears. I also saw a kingfisher dive for a fish and a mink swam across the stream while covys of quail and grouse rose from the banks. We had to pass through two small rapids and after the last of these we pitched our tents by another and much larger one, down which only one of our guides attempted to go and he sprung a leak in his boat. On the way we caught eight trout and we had them for supper. After supper Father read aloud to us from *The Last of the Mohicans.* In the middle of the reading I fell asleep. Father read by the light of the campfire.

In the bush, August 9th/71: West, Jake [Hayes, a guide] and I went fishing before breakfast and Jake caught six trout. After breakfast West and I waded through the rapids fishing but caught no fish. Jake and Ellie went up stream and Father and Godfry down stream. These brought in about two dozen trout.

After dinner all of us began to whip' the rapids. At first I sat on a rock by the water but the black flies drove me from there, so I attempted to cross the rapids. But I had miscalculated my strength, for before I was half way across the force of the current had swept me into water, which was above my head. Leaving the pole to take [care] of itself, I struck out for a rock. My pole soon stuck and so I recovered it. I then went half-wading, half-swimming down stream, fishing all the time but unsuccessful. West and Ellie were equally unsuccessful, but Father caught two and the guides a good many.[3]

Herbert Hoover loved to fish, starting with his boyhood rambles in rural Iowa and Oregon. In his book *Fishing for Fun,* he described some of these joys.

I was a boy in the days before civilization became so perfect, before it was paved with cement and made of bricks. Boys were not so largely separated from Mother Nature and all her works. And that was before the machine age denied them their natural rights as primitive, combative animals to match their wits with birds and animals. . . .

The most vivid and joyous recollections of my Iowa boyhood days are of patient angling in Iowa streams for the very occasional fish, with a willow pole and a properly spat-upon worm. . . .

In 1907 President Theodore Roosevelt went on a fishing and hunting trip to Louisiana. In a drawing to his son Archie, he captured Dr. Alexander Lambert pulling in "a good many bass." Lambert was the family physician and a long-time friend of Roosevelt. Letters to His Children. *New York: Scribners, 1919, p. 213.*

One time, in the spring, our grandmothers used to give us nasty brews from sulphur and herbs to purify our blood of the winter's coruptions. They knew something was the matter with the boys. They could have saved trouble by giving them a pole, a string, and a hook. Some wise ones—among them my own— did just that. . . .

When I was ten years old, I was transported to Oregon. Oregon lives in my mind for its gleaming wheat fields, its abundant fruits, its luxuriant forest vegetation, and the fish in the mountain streams. To step into its forests with their tangle of berry bushes, their ferns, their masses of wild flowers, stirs up odors peculiar to Oregon. Within these woods are never-ending journeys of discovery, and the hunts for grouse and expeditions for trout.

There was not so much water in proportion to the fish then, and legal limits had not been thought of. I, like other boys, fished with worms until a generous fisherman, whom we met during an excursion to the upper Santiam, gave four of us three artificial flies each. They proved powerfully productive. It never occurred to me that they were perishable. In any event, I nursed those three flies and used them until all the feathers were worn off—and still the trout rose to them.[4]

In the same book, Hoover recounted an apocryphal story attributed to him:

I was supposed to be returning after a day's fishing without a single fish when I met a boy who was toting home a beautiful catch.

I asked: "Where did you get them?"

He said: "You just walk down that lane marked Private till you come to a sign that says Trespassers Will Be Prosecuted. Just beyond is a stream marked No Fishing Allowed, and there you are."[5]

In 1955, three years into Dwight Eisenhower's first term, writer Ed Mason, in *Rod and Gun* magazine, explored the angling roots of the "nation's Most Noted Fisherman":

He has been scattering reporters and photographers with his backcasts since before World War II. He has hardly wet a line in the past decade without somebody recording the event on film. Where he's fishing, what he's catching, how he cooks 'em— everybody knows the intimate details nowadays.

But where were his fisherman's hankerings born?

Were there favorite spots where young Ike learned the special thrill that a taut line and a jiggling pole transmit to hand and arm and heart? Do small fry and teenagers still work over the same old fishing holes? What do they catch there today?

There is a lot of the typical American boy in the president's fishing history. We see him pictured now in the rushing streams of the scenic Rockies, with split bamboo and dry fly to tempt the wary rainbows; but his first fishing trips were not so glamorous. They show a small boy hoofing it down the Santa Fe tracks in Abilene, Kansas, seven blocks to Mud Creek.

His tackle was regulation stuff—a willow shoot, a length of

stout string, a five-cent hook from the general store. His bait, of course, was a can of worms. He collected this bait the hard way, the by-product of hours on the business end of a hoe in the family corn patch. . . .[6]

The boys' catch included sunfish, bullheads, carp, and drum. Other favorite fishing spots for the Eisenhower boys and their friends were the Smokey Hill River and Lyons Creek, about twenty miles below Abilene.

In preparing material for this book, I wrote to every living president to ask about their early fishing experiences. President Ford replied with the following letter:

January 27, 1994
Dear Mr. Mares:

As a youngster I reluctantly fished because my Dad was an ardent fly fisherman for Michigan's trout and he always took me along. When I became old enough to play competitive team sports I lost all interest in fishing. Much to Dad's disappointment.

On rare occasions I've done some ocean fishing, but without success. Also, as a good father I took our four young children fishing off the piers in Lake Michigan. They inherited my lack of enthusiasm.

Sorry I can't help you on the affirmative side. Nevertheless, good luck.
Regards,
(signed)
Gerald R. Ford

George Bush did his earliest fishing on and off the coast of Maine, where the family had a retreat at Kennebunkport. It was exclusively salt-water fishing. He discussed this experience in an interview in the April 1989 issue of *Fly Rod & Reel*.

"I started fishing at age five or so. [My] earliest recollection is catching mackerel on a lead jig with piece of white cloth for bait . . . trolling with that old green cotton line."

The trolling was in a converted lobster boat called the *Tom Boy*, which was owned by his grandfather Walker.

"I also fished off the Maine rocks for pollock [greasy, inedible devils] and for cunner, a brown spiny-backed inedible fish. We'd also get the occasional small flounder, and I loved jigging for smelt."

Dwight Eisenhower camping along the Smokey Hill River south of Abilene with friends, sometime between 1904 and 1907. EISENHOWER PRESIDENTIAL LIBRARY.

Those "Maine rocks" that Bush and his buddies used to clamber over were at Walker Point. They'd add lead to the line and fish off the bottom or "cast" the heavy line and its double hooks and then slowly retrieve them.[7]

In his sporting memoir, *An Outdoor Journal,* Jimmy Carter recalls that all his early fishing companions were black, with the finest being Rachel, who showed him how to get up the "branches" to fish, starting with cane poles, five-mile walks, and moving up the ladder from catfish to sunfish and bass. Sometimes they would fish all night, setting up with coffee and grits and a lantern to draw the eels. On special occasions Jimmy would join the stampede to gig spotted suckers as the fish swam up small streams to spawn. "Sometimes it was possible to straddle the entire current with a foot planted firmly on each bank. Shining a flashlight beam down into the water, we tried to spear the fast-moving fish as they went by. . . . We thought ourselves lucky if, after hours of effort, we got two or three of them." Carter acknowledged that he was never a very good sucker

Gerald "Junior" Ford appeared with a side-show fish as an eighteen-month-old in 1915.
GERALD R. FORD LIBRARY.

Gerald Ford and his cousin Gardner James show off the day's catch on an unidentified dock, c. 1923. GERALD R. FORD LIBRARY.

fisherman, but "for a boy, such fishing was a real adventure, combining secrecy and intrigue, the patience of waiting until there was a prospective catch, a special technique, the power of the hooked fish, and the enjoyment of the resulting meal."[8]

Carter described the great joy of receiving his first bait-casting outfit, a hard-earned four-foot-long Shakespeare rod and a Pflueger reel. With that equipment and a bicycle and a tackle box of Jitterbugs, Hawaiian Wigglers, and other lures, a new horizon dawned. He would go fishing with his friends to nearby ponds and sloughs and with his father to the distant Okefenokee Swamp in southeast Georgia. They caught perch and catfish and bass and even the fearsome-looking primordial alligator gar.

> Then came my most memorable day. Late one afternoon,
> after a good day of fishing, Daddy called me over and asked me
> to keep his string while he went up the river to talk to one of

his friends. I tied it on with mine on the downstream side of me while I kept fishing, enjoying the steady pull of the current on our day's catch. It wasn't long before I watched my cork begin to move slowly and steadily up under a snag and knew I had hooked a big one. After a few minutes I had a large copperhead bream in my hands, but as I struggled with it and wondered how I was going to hold the fish while untying the stringer, a chill went down my spine. I realized that the tugging of the current on the stringers was gone, as were all our fish! My belt loop had broken.

I threw my pole up on the nearest sandbar and began to dive madly into the river below where I had been standing.

Then I heard Daddy's voice calling my nickname. "Hot," he said. "What's wrong?"

"I've lost the fish, Daddy."

"All of them? Mine, too?"

"Yes sir." I began to cry, and the tears and water ran down my face together each time I came up for breath.

Daddy was rarely patient with foolishness or mistakes. But after a long silence, he said, "Let them go." I stumbled out on the bank, and he put his arms around me.

It seems foolish now, but at that time it was a great tragedy for me. We stood there for a while, and he said, "There are a lot more fish in the river. We'll get them tomorrow." He knew how I felt and was especially nice to me for the next couple of days. I worshipped him.[9]

CHAPTER THREE

FISHING ON THE JOB/FISHING FOR A JOB[1]

This campaign will be settled on fish. Do you want a deep sea fisherman in the White House—flounders and cod—or a big trout and perch man?
—*Will Rogers (1932)*

There are a dozen justifications for fishing. Among them is its importance to the political world. No political aspirant can qualify for election unless he demonstrates he is a fisherman, there being twenty-five million persons who pay annually for a license to fish.
—*Herbert Hoover*

The press loved to get as close to our boat as they could. They'd be in so tight it was like trying to troll in a Mixmaster.
—*George Bush*[2]

A few years ago," wrote former President Herbert Hoover in the 1950s, "a press photograph showed my friend the late Senator Robert Taft awkwardly holding a common fish. It was taken from many angles, for all the common men to see. I knew without other evidence that he was a candidate."[3] As it turned out, Taft was not much of a fisherman, nor a national candidate, and he lost the Republican nomination to Dwight Eisenhower, an accomplished fly fisherman.

Over the last hundred-plus years, the intensification of public interest in presidential activities, official and otherwise, has grown into an obsession. At the same time, presidents and candidates have increasingly played to this public fascination.

This chapter deals with what might be called the public side of presidential fishing. As the presidents and candidates have increasingly built their campaigns and governance on image and perception, they have used every conceivable device and occasion to influence public attitudes and

BAITIN' FOR "IKE"

In mid-1951, both parties were hoping that retired general Dwight Eisenhower would show his true partisan colors and be their candidate. Ike, then president of Columbia University, played it coy in this cartoon by Ed Kuekes. CLEVELAND PLAIN-DEALER.

Whose Fish?

By the next year, Ike had become a Republican and he battled Senator Robert Taft for delegates to the convention. FRED O. SEIBEL PAPERS, SPECIAL COLLECTIONS DEPARTMENT, UNIVERSITY OF VIRGINIA LIBRARY.

opinions, including sports and recreation. As Hoover so bluntly pointed out, it was a foolish presidential aspirant who neglected twenty-five million voter/anglers.

The evolution of fishing as a political ploy and a public interest was gradual, in part because not every president fished. More importantly, as Professor Gil Troy has shown in his excellent volume *See How They Ran,* presidential candidates did not even campaign until late in the nineteenth century. Candidates "stood" for office. The whole notion of candidates running or stumping for office was considered offensive to a population that still saw the president as far above the fray.[4]

The third party to this transformation was the press/media. Presidents and candidates could only meet a tiny fraction of the populace, but increasingly gossipy newspapers and now ubiquitous television cameras could bring the president into the living room. The public had a growing appetite for seeing the president throw out the first pitch of the baseball season or playing golf with celebrities.

The angling equivalent of kissing babies and photo opportunities was to cast a line for the press's lenses—and the public's approval. Fishing humanized the presidents and candidates. Anglers were a voting block not to be scorned, perhaps the second largest after the elderly. After all, in the 1990s there are over sixty-five million licensed anglers, more than two and one-half times the number in Hoover's day.

The stories here offer presidents and candidates in a variety of venues, fishing either in the public eye or with a public purpose. The first records some angling by George Washington. In 1789, the new President took a month-long journey to New England to see and be seen. As biographer James Flexner wrote, "He wished to become familiar anew with an area he had known only in wartime, and to make, in this powerful part of the nation, the federal government visible."[5] In New Hampshire he made a stop in Portsmouth. He recorded in his diary:

> 2 November 1789: Portsmouth, N.H. Having made previous preparations for it—About 8 O'clock attended by the President [of the state, General Sullivan], Mr. Langden & some other Gentlemen—I went in a boat to view the harbour of Portsmouth, which is well secured against all Winds; and from its narrow entrance from the Sea, and passage up to the Town, may be perfectly guarded against any approach by water. The anchorage is also good & the Shipping may lay close to the

Docks &ca. when at the Town. In my way to the Mouth of the Harbour, I stopped at a place called Kittery in the Provence of Main, [sic] the River Piscataqua being the boundary between New Hampshire and it. From hence I went by the Old Fort [built while under the former English government] on an Island which is at the Entrance of the Harbour and where the Light House stands. As we passed this Fort we were saluted by 13 Guns. Having lines, we proceeded to the Fishing Banks a little without the Harbour and fished for Cod. But it was not being a proper time of tide; we only caught two, with wh'ch, about 1 o'clock, we returned to Town. Dined at Mr. Landon's and drank Tea there, with a large circle of Ladies, and retired a little after seven o'clock. . . .[6]

And of those two fish, one wasn't even his own, for as a local newspaper account told it, "Zebulon Willey, who was fishing in the vicinity—finding them toiling in vain—had hooked a cod, and coming along side, handed his line to the President, who drew up the prize. This was a good pull for Zebulon, for the President gave him a silver dollar—and the story was a golden one for him ever after."[7]

CHESTER ARTHUR HELPS TO SAVE YELLOWSTONE PARK
In 1883, eleven years after the opening of Yellowstone National Park in the Wyoming Territory—the first national park in the world—President Chester A. Arthur made a 350-mile fishing and hunting trip through its magnificence. The spectacular geysers, falls, vistas, and animal herds, which had caught the eyes of visitors and photographers for years, had moved Congress to preserve natural beauty.

Instrumental in the trip were General Phil Sheridan and Senator George Vest of Missouri. Both men were dedicated to protecting the new national park from commercial exploitation. They believed that they could solidify the President's support best by taking him there. Intrigued, Arthur accepted their invitation and bought a variety of new fishing tackle. The party rode from Fort Washakie through the Upper and Lower Geyser basins, camping by trout streams every night. No reporters were allowed, for as Sheridan noted, "If we have a newspaperman along, our pleasure will be destroyed." The party of ten was accompanied by a seventy-five-man escort of cavalry with 174 pack animals, and an elaborate system of couriers was established. The party rode between fifteen and twenty miles each day, and the President and his companions fished almost every day.[8]

The photographer F. Jay Haynes accompanied President Arthur's expedition to Yellowstone Park in August 1883. Among those pictured here are General Phil Sheridan (third from left), then Secretary of War (and President Lincoln's son) Robert Lincoln. President Arthur sits on the chair in the background. HAYNES FOUNDATION COLLECTION, MONTANA HISTORICAL SOCIETY.

The President and Vest were both accomplished anglers. Indeed, Vest later wrote that Arthur's "array of tackle was enough to bewilder an entire fishing club." And yet for all that equipment, neither man was able to catch as many fish as the soldiers and mule drivers kept snaring with jury-rigged twine, poles, and grasshoppers. Arthur deputed Vest to learn their technique.

> Not believing the antiquated absurdity that the average country lad with a hoop pole and rusty hook can vanquish the true angler with his six-ounce bamboo, oiled line, and leader, supplemented by well-made flies, I determined to investigate the puzzling and mortifying results before mentioned . . . when I saw the caution with which they crawled around the rocks and bushes, stealthily dropping their bait into eddies made by the rapid current, and then yanking the wary trout out of the water without a second's delay, the mystery was fully explained.[9]

Some of Arthur's catch displayed on a string with accompanying fishing rod. HAYNES
FOUNDATION COLLECTION, MONTANA HISTORICAL SOCIETY.

President Arthur and members of the expedition seated outside tents near the Snake River with the Teton Mountains in the distance. HAYNES FOUNDATION COLLECTION, MONTANA HISTORICAL SOCIETY.

Thereafter the pair's success improved dramatically, and on one day the two of them caught 105 pounds of trout.

Eugene Field, a Chicago poet who used his doggerel to prick various social and political pretensions, captured a moment after the President had left, in a poem called "The Indian and the Trout":

> The morning sun in splendor shone
> On the mellow park of the Yellowstone.
> The President at the break of day
> Had packed his duds and moved away.
> A brave Shoshone chief came out
> With his willow pole to fish for trout.
> It was half-past six when he cast his line,
> And he kept on fishing till half-past nine;
> And then he baited his hook anew
> And patiently fished until half-past two—
> Then meanwhile swearing a powerful sight
> For fishing all day with nary a bite.

And he swore and fished, and fished and swore
Til his Elgin watch tolled half-past four;
When a big, fat trout came swimming by
And winked at the chief with his cold, sad eye.

"And do you reckon, you pagan soul,
You can catch us trout with a willow pole?
The President taught us manners while
He fished for us in the latest style.
You've no idea how proud we feel
To be jerked ashore with a Frankfort reel!"

The red man gathered his dinner pail
And started home by the shortest trail,
And he told his faithful squaw he guess'd
They'd better move still further west,
Where presidents didn't come fooling about,
Turning the heads of the giddy trout.[10]

Most importantly, Vest and Sheridan had accomplished their main purpose. Through the widespread publicity that attended the trip, public support for park preservation was solidified, and the first national park in the world was protected for future generations.

FISHING ON HIS HONEYMOON

Grover Cleveland was one of the most fervent anglers who ever occupied the Oval Office. Indeed, in 1886, after he was married in the White House, he took his fly rods on the honeymoon. He had rented a cottage in western Maryland that had well-stocked trout pools, remarking, "If I am going to keep my reputation as a fisherman, I must go where there are plenty of trout."[11] Unfortunately, he had not counted on the journalistic black flies who would plague his idyll.

Their curiosity was unlimited. They pursued the bridal pair by train, horse, and foot. For six days the reporters kept watch just beyond the private guards and Secret Service, reporting every snippet of public activity of the President and First Lady, be it strolling, cigar smoking, fishing, or going to church. Cleveland was enraged at these intrusions, and in a letter to the *New York Evening Post* he condemned the correspondents who have "used the enormous power of the modern newspaper to perpetuate and disseminate a colossal impertinence, and have done it, not as professional gossips and tattlers, but as the guides and instructors of the public in conduct and morals."[12]

Cleveland would henceforth do most of his fishing near his summer house on Buzzards Bay in Massachusetts.

WITH FRIENDS LIKE THESE . . .

As if Cleveland didn't have enough worries about the press, he was betrayed by his own secretary, serving as a press officer. Early in his second term, the President sneaked away for a fishing vacation in Virginia. He told the secretary, Henry T. Thurber, not to reveal his whereabouts. While he was gone, a prominent citizen died, and the reporters pressed Thurber for the President's reaction. Thurber held the press at bay in a White House anteroom while he went into the President's office, presumably to query the chief executive. A few moments later Thurber emerged to say that the President had been moved to tears at news of the man's death and that the nation had undoubtedly suffered a grievous loss. The next day, however, these stories appeared side by side with dispatches from Virginia reporting the President's journey home from his angling trip.[13]

Much later, Cleveland would write, "[W]hen short fishing excursions, in which I have sought relief from the wearing labors and perplexities of official duty, have been denounced in a mendacious newspaper as dishonest devices to cover scandalous revelry, I have been able to enjoy a sort of pleasurable contempt for the author of these accusations, while congratulating myself on the mental and physical restoration I have derived from these excursions."[14]

TWO WARNINGS NOT TO FISH

In the election of 1888, neither President Cleveland nor his Republican opponent, Benjamin Harrison, did much campaigning. Harrison would stroll out to a local park near his Indiana home and make an occasional speech. His handlers tried to make him more appealing by publicizing some personal facts about him—his hat and shoe size, the price of his shirts and suits, and his favorite sports of fishing and baseball[15]—but he was warned against making a public display of angling. "For God's sake, Benjamin," a Kansas politician wrote, "do not get a fishing reputation at the start . . . take a fool's advice, and watch public opinion, and let Grover Cleveland go fishing."[16] Harrison won, and like Cleveland, he did not invite the press on his subsequent occasional fishing vacations to the Adirondacks.

A line drawing of Cleveland by Henry Watson, probably copied from a photograph of the retired President when he was vacationing near Tamworth, N.H. THE OUTING PUBLISHING COMPANY.

Coincidentally, in this same year 1888, George Eastman brought out the Kodak camera, which brought photography to the masses. According to Susan Kismaric in her study of American political photographs, "For the first time, a politician could be photographed by the very people he represented. . . . The development of this more flexible photographic technology helped to reinforce the politician's association with popular values . . . which may or may not reflect a politician's actual inclinations."[17] It would be some years before those cameras were turned on presidential fishing for the simple reason that between Cleveland and Harding, few presidents fished in public or private. But the camera would bring all presidential activities that much closer to the public's everyday activities.

Perhaps more than any president, Theodore Roosevelt transformed the nature of presidential campaigning. He dominated every election between 1900 and 1912. He stumped relentlessly whether in office or out of it. In 1908 he campaigned hard for his chosen successor, William Howard Taft (Robert's father). However, he cautioned Taft not to publicize his recreational activities. "I hope your people will do everything they can to prevent one word being sent out about either your fishing or your playing golf. The American people regard the campaign as a very serious business, and we want to be careful that your opponents do not get the chance to misrepresent you as not taking it with sufficient seriousness. . . ."[18]

Roosevelt's successors turned a deaf ear to such advice. They had to go where the votes and people were. Taft would establish the enduring tradition that the president threw out the first baseball on opening day.[19]

It's worth pointing out that although Roosevelt didn't fish very much as an adult, he had a profound influence on the fishing of later generations. As fly-fishing historian Paul Schullery has written,

> Even if Roosevelt had never fished in his life, all anglers would still owe him an enormous debt for his role in the progressive conservation movement at the turn of the century. With expert advisors such as Gifford Pinchot [Roosevelt's chief forester], Roosevelt conducted a far-reaching campaign to protect and better manage all kinds of natural resources, from sea birds to watersheds, from archaeological sites to elk.[20]

HARDING "SACRIFICES A FISH TO ART"[21]

As a senator, Warren Harding had fished with his senatorial cronies several times. After his easy victory over Democrat James M. Cox in 1920,

Cartoonist Clifford Berryman has Harding reminding himself that losing a tarpon still pales by comparison with winning the presidency and the Congress. THE U.S. SENATE COLLECTION, CENTER FOR LEGISLATIVE ARCHIVES.

Harding headed to Texas for some golf and fishing. He didn't mind having the press follow him, but he told them that politics and assembling a cabinet were taboo on the trip; the only problem he would face willingly was whether to fish in the morning and play golf in the afternoon or vice versa. On this trip he would meet with Frank Scobey, the clerk of the Senate, and Gus Creager, an oilman, land speculator, and influential Texas Republican from south Texas. Also along was Senator Frederick Hale of Maine.

Each day he went fishing, Harding drew a crowd of spectators and the press with their many cameras. Off Point Isabel, Texas, Hale was the first to catch a fish, while Harding looked on enviously. Shortly thereafter, the President-elect had a strike, and for the next forty-five minutes, Harding and his Mexican boatman fought the tarpon's leaps and runs, first gaining ground, then losing it again. The fish began to show signs of exhaustion.

At this moment some news cameramen begged Harding to pull the fish closer to the shore for better pictures. The weary Harding complied, and in calmer waters he set out to restage the struggle for the newsmen.

Alas, the calm waters also gave the tarpon a breather, and it lit out for the pilings of an abandoned wharf. Several Coast Guardsmen cried out a warning, but it was too late. The fish reached the pilings and wound the line around a rock. One of the Coast Guardsmen leaped into the water fully clothed to unsnag the line, but just at that moment the fish broke the line and leaped to freedom.

This was Harding's only strike that day, but he put on a brave face and announced that the catch had been "sacrificed to art."

The next day he did catch a four-foot six-inch tarpon, and even the *New York Times* gushed:

> While probably he will make no mention of it in his formal address at tomorrow's Armistice Day celebration at Brownsville, and while he refuses to be drawn at present into any speculation over foreign relations, politics or cabinet making, Senator Harding unquestionably believes in the freedom of the seas, provided the seas are free with fish and particularly generous with the viciously fighting silver-scaled tarpon in the swift current of Pass Brazos de Santiago.[22]

COOLIDGE CATCHES TWO ON ONE LINE

Cautious in angling as in most things, Calvin Coolidge was leery of letting the press and public see him fishing. Although he would report his catches when it suited him, he rarely allowed the press to see him actually fish. However, he seems to have pulled out all stops on his fifty-sixth birthday (July 4, 1928) when he vacationed on the Brule River in northern Wisconsin. He had long since told the nation that he did "not choose to run," and the Republicans had nominated Herbert Hoover as their candidate at a convention that Coolidge chose not to attend. But on that day he allowed newsreel cameramen and still photographers to crowd the shores and even board boats to record his piscatorial prowess.

To everyone's surprise, in the first fifteen minutes Coolidge pulled out not one but two hefty trout on one cast. At first there were skeptical guffaws that this was too neat, too pat. But then the Chippewa guide, John Laroque, said that the reason was simple—Coolidge had been fishing with two different flies, a Royal Coachman and a Black Gnat. That led the reporters to ask about a three-and-a-half pounder Coolidge had allegedly

President Coolidge fishes in a small brook near the family homestead in Plymouth Notch, Vermont, in this undated photo. COURTESY VERMONT HISTORICAL SOCIETY, MONTPELIER.

caught several days earlier. As if on cue, Laroque pulled the fish out of a box in the canoe, and the President manfully held it up for the press to acknowledge. After the two-fish success, Coolidge caught four more trout. But then his luck changed, and after an hour of fruitless casting, Coolidge and Laroque headed for a birthday party on the lawn in front of the cabin. Coolidge shared the cake and cigars with the press.[23]

HOOVER FISHES FOR VOTES

By the time he ran for president, Herbert Hoover was well-known as an accomplished fresh- and salt-water angler. He had been president of the Izaak Walton League and delivered a famous speech "On Disappearing Game Fish" that proposed a triage system for saving fishing waters. During his 1928 campaign, Hoover took time off to fish for steelhead on the Rogue River at a camp belonging to "Toggery Bill" Issacs, a Medford, Oregon, haberdasher. The camp was comfortable, without telephone—but also without fish. As the *New York Herald Tribune* reported, liberally interpolating the candidate's feelings, Hoover had a "fairly well-confirmed faith that he would have no luck since he had heard before of the big runs of steelhead and had failed to find them. . . . [Fishing the next day on the Klamath River was] much nearer Mr. Hoover's idea of the sport, anyway, than is angling along the Rogue. A large element of the fun to Mr. Hoover is being able to smoke a pipe, fish quietly, enjoy nature, talk a little, and reflect upon matters generally. Fishing in the turbulent Rogue requires wading in rubber boots in swift currents waist-deep and over slippery rocks. Keeping one's equilibrium in the Rogue is a large part of the undertaking. So much labor for so little results is not altogether to the Hoover taste."[24]

WILL ROGERS, FISH, AND THE 1932 ELECTION

Once in office, Herbert Hoover had less than a year for untrammeled public fishing before the Great Depression struck. Beset by problems he could not solve nor even encompass, Hoover retreated to his Rapidan River camp almost every weekend. He did almost no public fishing. Still, the voters so identified both Hoover and his opponent, Franklin D. Roosevelt, with fishing that Will Rogers, America's Everyman, could write in July 1932:

> Roosevelt has actually started his Presidential campaign. I see pictures all over the front page today of him fishing. Are we never to get an original candidate?

Well at least he dident [sic] stand in the creek with rubber boots on. This campaign will be settled on fish. Do you want a deep-sea fisherman in the White House—flounders and cod— or a big trout and perch man?[25]

Four months later, on the eve of the election, after watching the mudslinging, Rogers told the candidates to take a break:

You boys just get the weight of the world off your shoulders and go fishing. Both of you claim you like to fish; now, instead of calling each other names 'til next Tuesday, why, you can do everybody a big favor and go fishing, and you will be surprised but the old U.S. will keep right on running while you boys are on the bank. Then come back next Wednesday, and we will let you know which one is the lesser of two evils to us.[26]

FDR'S MOST EMBARRASSING FISHING TRIP

Public interest in Franklin D. Roosevelt's fishing naturally intensified once he was elected. Such attention led to acute embarrassment in 1933. He was fishing aboard the *Amberjack II* off New England while boatloads of Secret Service agents and the press followed. Everywhere the President moved on the boat, he had to be carried. It was especially difficult getting down the narrow passageways, which he had to traverse several times a day to relieve himself.

This was an awkward business; it is not easy to carry a six-foot-three, 190-pound man in narrow quarters. It was hard work for those doing the carrying, and it was uncomfortable and undignified for the one being carried. So it was not surprising one foggy morning, as son James recounts, that Roosevelt "suggested that, in light of the special circumstances of fog, a triangular extension of the stern could perhaps serve as a toilet seat; he could simply do what had to be done right there." With the President thus positioned, James went up to the flying bridge to give his father privacy.

"No sooner had I reached the bridge," said James, "than I realized the fog was lifting. And there coming asteaming up on us, were several ships of the convoy. As they closed in, Father was bound to be visible. I shouted a warning." Shouting for his brothers belowdecks, James rushed to his father. "They can't see the President like this," said FDR. With that, FDR's sons picked him up, with his pants down, and hustled him down the companionway.[27]

FDR brought a much more relaxed demeanor to presidential fishing. Here he poses next to the 260-pound shark he caught off the Cocos Islands, August 1, 1938. FRANKLIN D. ROOSEVELT LIBRARY.

Undaunted by this close brush, Roosevelt continued to fish frequently. Perhaps inevitably, that fishing became a political issue. In the 1936 campaign, Republicans shelled him with the slogan: Give me a fishing pole and call me Roosevelt! Unfortunately for them, it didn't work, and Roosevelt rolled over Alf Landon of Kansas.

That same year, brilliant and acerbic columnist for the *New York Herald Tribune,* Dorothy Thompson, noting the lengthening shadow of Hitler and Mussolini, penned an enthusiastic and witty defense of fishing as the sport of democrats.[28]

> I should like to call attention to a far more subtle, far more dangerous piece of campaign propaganda, this time from the Democrats. It consists of drawing not a red herring, but a Middle Bight bonefish across the trail of national issues. In the midst of a debate on the new taxation bill in which the Administration has received the embarrassing kiss of the Communist party; in the

midst of [Agriculture] Secretary Wallace's unwilling revelations that among the destitute farmers whom the American taxpayer [has] been saving from starvation are Florida, Puerto Rico, and Hawaii sugar companies, the President has been fishing.

Now, it is one of the most impregnable traditions of the great republic that all fishermen are safe, sane fellows. Not only are they incapable of harm to anything except a fly or a fish, but they are sounder, mellower, and more profoundly learned than any other breed of humans. From Izaak Walton to Henry van Dyke, a literature has been built up, which has become part of the unconscious public mind, that a man who fishes is a conserver of all the pious virtues. It would be safer to attack the Y.M.C.A., the sanctity of motherhood, the histrionic genius of Shirley Temple, the superiority of pipe-smokers to cigarette puffers, or even the nobility of dogs than to attack the honesty, incorruptibility and gentle humorous wisdom of a fisherman.

As long as the President is fishing, dark omens of impending dictatorship will fade. Whoever heard of a dictator who was a fisherman? Mussolini plays the violin and rides horseback, but so did Nero. Hitler loves dogs, but so did Napoleon. Stalin has a good press in an anti-communist world. Why? Because he smokes a pipe all the time, ruminatively, and even that intrepid pursuer of the neuroses of dictators, Mr. John Gunther, is mollified. Stalin, he thinks must be a good common-sense fellow after all. But none of these gentlemen would think of posing as fishermen. The Austrian Emperor Franz Josef held together a decaying empire for fifty years, merely by hunting chamois. When there was a crisis with the Croats or the Serbs, he went out in a green hat with a brush in it, in leather pants and embroidered suspenders, and hunted chamois, and to this day, and for this reason, the Austrians have an international reputation for being kind and good, gay and irresponsible, fond of children, women, and song, even as they establish concentration camps and summarily hang their political opponents. Hunting the chamois is the Austrian equivalent of hunting the fish. Ours is the Anglo-Saxon tradition. Has no one observed that whenever a cabinet crisis occurs in Great Britain, the Prime Minister rushes to Scotland and catches a salmon? Then the fears of the public are allayed. All is quiet; the outlook is serene; conditions may be serious but not hopeless.

All things being equal, a fishing candidate has an immense break over a non-fisherman. Coolidge fished, Hoover fished in half-hearted way, Grover Cleveland was the very type of a fisherman-statesman. But none of them, as far as records available to me show, ever landed a Middle Bight or any other sort of bonefish.[29] This is fishing in the grand manner. This is a thousand dollar fish, so called, I take it, because it costs that much to catch one. Why should anyone, then, worry about the unbalanced budget?

It is a most subtle blow against the other possible Presidential candidates. Has any one ever heard of Idaho's [Senator William] Borah catching fish? I have seen [Michigan's] Senator [Arthur] Vandenberg's Washington home and never seen so much as a stuffed glazed and mounted two-pound black bass. If Dickinson and [eventual Republican vice-presidential candidate Frank] Knox have trophies, they should prepare to show them now. As for Landon, what are his opportunities in Topeka? He might snare baby perch in one of the drainage canals. Possibly all these men are fishermen. If they are, the time has come for their managers to exploit this fact.

For not only are fishermen inevitably believed to be patient philosophers, loftily elevated to Buddha-like wisdom above the strife of classes and parties, but they are known to choose as their counselors simple honest souls whose prototype is the Maine guide. A good smoky, rugged, tanned, tobacco-scented Maine guide. If fiction reveals that he is a poker player, he is presented as nature's gentleman, graciously willing to leave his fellows a portion of their shirts. A friend of Maine guides is invariably a friend of the people. And the Maine guide is merely the symbol of fishermen's guides everywhere.

And yet where is the completely convincing non-circumstantial evidence that the Chief Executive has ever really caught a fish? He is surrounded by picked and trusted guards, by aides, by press agents. Is there a single objective witness who can testify that the tarpon or bonefish [was] dragged from the deeps by his own hand? Even the dispatches are guarded in reporting this significant detail. When the Austrian monarchy fell, revolutionary souls stepped forward to destroy its glamour and prestige. And it was publicly avowed that not all the antlers decorating the hunting lodges of the Habsburgs were the fruits of the royal rifle. It was hinted that the chamois miraculously fell simultaneously with the report of his majesty's gun but that the cartridges in their hides did not always correspond to those in the imperial pockets. This revelation, true or false, marked the final decline of a thousand years of sovereignty.

It is possible, of course, that with the bonefish the President has overreached himself. There is something strong, foreign, fantastic, and ominous about a bonefish. It is not one of the most neighborly fishes. The wily trout of the New England stream can comfortably be associated with Coolidge and safety. The bass of the Great Lakes is indubitably American. But these fish of the Bahamas are fishes of foreign, of international, waters. They are not the fish to which one is accustomed. They are not even every fisherman's fishes. What manner of creature is the President landing on our shores? It sounds fishy.

On the eve of World War II, historian Dixon Wechter noted that American democracy demanded a special breed of hero.

> [U]nlike the Stuarts, Bourbons, and Napoleons of the Old World [this hero] cannot invite public opinion to go to hell. . . . It likes to think of its idol as simple in greatness. Manliness, forthright manners, and salty speech are approved. Love of the soil, of dogs and horses, and manual hobbies and fishing is better understood than absorption in art, literature, and music. . . . The public distrusts Presidents who are photographed fishing in their street clothes.[30]

Herbert Hoover would be the last president to fish in a three-piece suit—indeed, in a coat and tie. The sartorial Democrats would carry the day.

Herbert Hoover almost never went fishing without a jacket and tie. NATIONAL ARCHIVES.

HARRY TRUMAN HIDES HIS DISTASTE

Harry Truman never had much love or aptitude for fishing. Poker, walking, telling stories were his real pleasures. On the other hand, Truman was a first-rate politician. And he knew the meaning of symbols, such as fishing, and he was willing to use those symbols as a way to reach voters.[31]

The photo on page 44 shows him fishing for sockeye salmon in Puget Sound in 1945 with Governor Wallgren of Washington. The party caught only two dogfish and had to accept a gift of salmon from more successful fishermen. If Truman was disappointed, you couldn't tell it from the photo.

The top photo on page 45 shows Truman as he began his extraordinary comeback in 1948. His approval ratings in the 20 percent range, Truman set off on a "non-political" swing through the West. Willing to use whatever tools were offered for the coming battle, he agreed to cast a line into Idaho's Green River for photographers. Although his attire was wildly inappropriate, his grin made up for it.

In the next photo, Truman holds up a Florida fish as proudly as he held up the *Chicago Tribune* edition erroneously showing Thomas Dewey

President Truman and Governor Mon Wallgren of Washington troll for salmon in Puget Sound in June 1945. Rowing the boat was fisheries executive Nick Bez. AP/WIDE WORLD PHOTOS.

the victor in 1948. According to Ken White, the Truman family photographer, Bess was a decidedly better angler than Harry, but he was the politician. The following is from an account in the *Kansas City Star:*

> One time I took Bess trout fishing. Well, Harry decided to go along because it would be a good chance for him to get out.
>
> Bess caught her limit of five trout—and they were nice ones—just like that. Bing, bing, bing. She handed him the rod and he said, no, he was just watching. I think he knew he had a pretty hard act to follow.
>
> Well, anyway, we had the fish on the stringer and I said, "Let's take a picture." He grabbed those fish and held them up real fast, and Bess was just left standing there off to the side. We all had to laugh about that one. He was a politician. He knew how to get those votes.[32]

Truman shows his novice fly-fishing form on the Green River in Idaho during his 1948 re-election campaign. COURTESY HARRY S TRUMAN LIBRARY.

Truman proudly displays the six-pound grouper which he caught off the Dry Tortugas in Florida in November 1946. COURTESY HARRY S TRUMAN LIBRARY.

NIXON THE INEPT

In the quiet moments before the beginning of the 1952 campaign, Dwight Eisenhower took a break for some fishing at the home of his friend Aksel Nielsen in Colorado. He took along his running mate, Richard Nixon. The famous Eisenhower grin, however, was conspicuously absent as Ike tried to teach Nixon the rudiments of fly-fishing while the press looked on. "It was a disaster," Nixon candidly recalled. "After hooking a limb the first three times, I caught his shirt on my fourth try. The lessons ended abruptly. I could see that he was disappointed because he loved fishing and could not understand why others did not like it as well as he did."[33]

Nixon *was* game. He tried fishing again three years later, when he went after snook in Florida with his friend Bebe Rebozo. *Sports Illustrated* sent along a reporter to document the outing.

> Richard Nixon's rapid rise from grocery clerk to Vice President of the United States left little time for play. Nixon did manage to find time in his packed schedule of governmental chores to get in some golf. But despite this enthusiastic excursion into the world of sport, in certain Washington quarters there still remained much shaking of heads and furrowing of brows as it was noted that the man only a heartbeat away from the Presidency did not know a Parmachene Belle from a backlash and seemingly cared less. Not since Calvin Coolidge supposedly donned white gloves and used hooks baited with worms by Secret Service men had there been a comparable crisis.
>
> But last week Dick Nixon journeyed to the Florida Everglades on a fishing expedition [that] included SI correspondent James Shepley. On his first attempt at the skilled sport of spincasting the Vice President threw out enough line for a bird's nest capable of housing a family of eagles. A companion cut away 50 yards of line and coached the novice. Gradually Nixon's technique improved, his enthusiasm soared. Suddenly, he snagged his line high in a mangrove. Struggling to get it loose, he jumped up on the skiff's seat and yanked. The skiff obeyed Newton's third law of motion and, like a skilled tumbler, Nixon did a neat back somersault over the gunwale. When he came up, he grabbed the side of the boat, and awkwardly climbed aboard. Damply returning to the sport, the conversion

Nixon doesn't show much enthusiasm for the fine points of fly-fishing during a vacation with Eisenhower in Fraser, Colorado, in July 1952. AP/WIDE WORLD PHOTOS.

Nixon puts on a game face after an unintended dousing while fishing in Florida. Stretching to unsnag a lure from a mangrove tree, he toppled into water. AP/WIDE WORLD PHOTOS.

appeared certain. But as the party headed home, the guide attempted a 180-degree turn. There was a sickening lurch, and Nixon, journalist Shepley, and guide found themselves in the Everglades mud. Aboard again, the Vice President of the United States finally found a proper parliamentary comment: "This certainly was an interesting experience."[34]

IKE CATCHES HIS LIMIT; PRESS CATCHES HELL

Early in his first term, Eisenhower went to State College, Pennsylvania, where his brother Milton was president of Pennsylvania State College. They did a little fishing in a nearby stream, but Ike was so hounded by kibitzers who importuned him with advice and angling devices that he fled to Colorado for most of his fishing.

There, when he fished at his friend Bal Swan's ranch, where the South Platte River ran close to a highway, people and press could park beside the road and observe the First Angler. If he wanted total privacy, he visited his friend Aksel Nielsen at the builder's Byers Peak Ranch, with its three miles of St. Louis River running through it.

In that summer of his first year as president (1953), Eisenhower invited several members of the press to observe his South Platte River fishing. Among them was Merriman Smith of United Press International. In a folksy, almost hagiographic volume called *Meet Mister Eisenhower,* Smith later told of Ike's personal activities and recreations such golfing, cooking, and painting. In a chapter entitled "On Calming Unquiet Thoughts," Smith recounted some of Ike's fishing experiences in Colorado.

He told of how Eisenhower was a good fly fisherman, but he was not so much of a purist that he refused to fish stocked streams *or* to use grasshoppers if artificial flies failed the test. In fact, he described how the President suddenly "dropped to his hands and knees and whipped off his blue hat. He crawled through the heavy grass like a man looking for a lost dime. Suddenly he spotted his quarry and began whacking the ground with his hat." After each whack he would reach under the hat to retrieve an insect.

On one of these trips, several newsmen gained permission from press secretary Jim Hagerty to fish, but at least a half mile up the South Platte from the President. To their surprise and delight, the pool they found on that hot day was apparently a haven for scores of stocked trout dumped in for Ike's benefit. The fish had no class and bit on every lure and technique

By fishing in public, presidents subjected themselves to kibitzers galore, as artist Carl Rose predicted in this preview of Eisenhower's trip to New England in June 1955.
COPYRIGHT 1955 BY THE *NEW YORK TIMES.* REPRINTED BY PERMISSION.

the journalists offered them . . . until Swan's ranch manager arrived in a rage. Apparently, the President wasn't catching anything, and the hosts didn't want the First Guest to hear that lowly reporters were taking fish reserved for the President.

On another count the reporters got themselves in hot water with the President. As normally happens with pool reporters (no pun intended), they shared their information about how the President had caught twelve fish. That was legal because the limit was twenty, according to a rule book at the ranch. And besides, the river was registered as a private stream, where the limits didn't apply. The pool reporters sent the report to their office in Denver, saying that the President had caught twelve fish, and thought no more about it.

Several hours later, the phones rang. The *Denver Post* had run a front-page story that if the President had caught twelve, he had broken the law because the legislature had lowered the limit to ten. When Smith and company checked the rule book, they found to their chagrin that it was out of date. What's more, they learned that the river's private registration had also lapsed. Sheepishly, the reporters approached Eisenhower. He was

In a few places, Ike was able to get away from the crowd of reporters and photographers. Here he brings a trout to net at Little Boy Falls on the Magalloway River in Maine.
DWIGHT D. EISENHOWER LIBRARY.

The press watches Ike fish in Maine. Ex-President Hoover once said he believed there were only two moments of solitude open to a president: fishing and prayer. After joining Eisenhower for some (public) angling, Hoover remarked that only prayer was left to him.
BUD LEAVITT PHOTO IN *FIELD & STREAM,* SEPTEMBER 1955.

incensed. He told them that he had caught his limit—period—and stalked off. It was left for Hagerty to take the fall and explain that the estimate had been in error.[35]

FISHING ON A "NON-POLITICAL" TRIP TO NEW ENGLAND

In June 1955, Eisenhower traveled to New England and fished in both Maine and Vermont. In neither place could he escape the minute examination of his techniques and catch (or lack of it).

At Little Boy Falls on the Magalloway River in northern Maine, Ike's hosts and guide made sure that he caught fish for the benefit of the scores of reporters and photographers who watched from the bank.

KENNEDY VS. DIEFENBAKER

In February 1961, shortly after his inauguration, John F. Kennedy received Prime Minister John Diefenbaker of Canada at the White House. They talked of a number of issues, such as Cuba, nuclear weapons, and trade. The two men would later become enemies, but at that moment they were just feeling each other out. According to Canadian journalist Knowlton Nash,

> Kennedy noted Diefenbaker's reputation as a fisherman and pointed to a stuffed sailfish on the wall of the White House "Fish Room" across the corridor from his office, asking, "Have

Jack Kennedy caught this sailfish on his honeymoon in Acapulco, Mexico, in 1953 but apparently did little or no fishing thereafter. COURTESY JOHN F. KENNEDY LIBRARY.

you ever caught anything better?" Kennedy had caught the sail-fish on his honeymoon in Acapulco. The prime minister glee-fully responded that he had just been in Jamaica, where he had caught a 140-pound, eight-and-a-half-foot marlin. It was some-thing of which he was inordinately proud, the biggest fish he had ever caught. But Kennedy teased him about it. "You didn't catch it," Diefenbaker remembered Kennedy saying. Diefen-baker replied that, yes, he had indeed pulled it in, and it had taken three hours and ten minutes to do it. "Well, that stuck in his craw," Diefenbaker later said.

When he got back to Ottawa, Diefenbaker made arrange-ments to have the marlin mounted on his office wall. "That bloody marlin was always staring at you," Diefenbaker aide Tommy Van Dusen says. "When [Kennedy] visited Canada," Diefenbaker later said, "one of the first things he said to me was, 'Where's your marlin?' When he saw it, he said, 'That is big.' And then he added something revealing: 'You know, I spent $50,000 trying to catch a fish like that'. . . . My catch did not cost me anything." It was a little triumph over Kennedy that Diefenbaker savoured all his life.[36]

CARTER'S STOLEN RODS

After Jimmy Carter was defeated by Ronald Reagan in 1980 and he had returned to Plains, Georgia, he discovered that two prized bamboo fly rods that he had been given during his presidency by a fishing organization had been stolen. One was given by the craftsmen at the H. L. Leonard Rod Company, while the other had come from an outdoor magazine for his role in protecting one hundred million acres of Alaska. The next time Carter went up to fish with his friend Wayne Harpster on Spruce Creek, his companions commiserated with him more about the loss of the rods than the election. In his book *An Outdoor Journal,* Carter wrote about the occasion, "Such were the important matters we discussed by the rich lime-stone waters of the Pennsylvania creek."[37]

SEVENTEEN FISHLESS DAYS

Probably no fishing president ever had as much public attention as George Bush. Part of that was caused by the place he chose to fish—Kenne-bunkport, Maine. He had grown up fishing there, and went back to the

After seventeen days without catching a fish in August and September 1989, President George Bush could be forgiven his evident glee at pulling in a ten-pound bluefish. "It was like a war was over," declared one observer. AP/WIDE WORLD PHOTOS.

family estate, the eight-acre peninsula of Walker Point. When he fished off the point, he had gawkers on three sides, and whenever he went out in his boat, *Fidelity,* he was surrounded by curiosity seekers, even though the Secret Service kept people three hundred to four hundred yards away. Bob Boilard, a local fishing guide and Bush friend, observed, "Whenever he went out, he had to run what I called Bush's Gauntlet. There were always ten or more boats around him—the Secret Service, communications boats, the press, public on-lookers. With that many boats, it scares the fish awful. I'd be out front catching fish, while Bush would be surrounded and not catching any fish. Finally, I told him: 'Mr. President, you have to get away from that armada, or you're not going to catch any fish.' And once he did that, he started catching fish."[38]

In the summer of 1989 Bush went to Kennebunkport for an eighteen-day vacation. Confidently, he predicted he would catch a bluefish before he returned to Washington. Day after day he went out with Boilard, and day after day he caught nothing. The *Portland Press Herald* began keeping a box on the front page, reminding readers of the number of presidential fishless days. Bush said several of his grandchildren got into the act and wrote up signs saying "You can do it" and "Go catch one" each day the President set off for the fishing grounds.[39]

(Bill and Carolyn Meub, friends of the author, were among that bevy of citizens who hovered near the President on one of those days. They were sailing, but they had some rods, so they decided to fish. Within thirty seconds they had hooked a bluefish; in the next hour and a half, they caught six more. Meanwhile, the President caught nothing. The Meubs were being shadowed by a Coast Guard cutter, and the sailors were laughing. The Meubs think that the reason they caught fish was that the armada of Secret Service craft, press boats, and citizens had simply frightened the fish away from Bush's boat *Fidelity,* and the pair were the beneficiaries.)[40]

Finally, on Bush's last day, a fish struck on a four-inch greenish "jaw-buster." When he pulled in the twenty-four-inch, ten-pound bluefish, it set off a cacophony of boat Klaxons, whistles, shouts, and cheers from people in nearby boats. Bush was ecstatic. He held the fish up as proud as any Wimbledon or Stanley Cup winner, then proceeded to clean it on the rocks of Walker Point. When presidential aides told reporters on land of Bush's success, Paul Bedard of the *New York Times* said it was "like the end of a war."[41]

Bush acknowledged that a president could be damned for both hyperactivity and sloth. In the early weeks of the Kuwait crisis of 1990, Bush was in residence at Kennebunkport, and one frequent visitor was National Security Adviser Brent Scowcroft. The President explained:

> We had discussions about Operation Desert Shield right out in my boat, *Fidelity.* He and I would go out there and talk. Oh, everyone was saying, "There they are fishing during this crisis." The press gave me a hard time about how I should be back in Washington managing this crisis. But I didn't want to scare the American public that summer by creating a crisis atmosphere. We knew what we had to do and were going to do. And the kinds of communications we had allowed us to conduct public business there. We even called the president of Syria from that boat.

Cartoonist Pat Oliphant may have been thinking of how Cleopatra sent divers down to put fish on Mark Antony's line in the Nile when he penned this drawing of Bush enduring day after day of fishless outings at Kennebunkport in the summer of 1989.

Was fishing a way to win votes? Bush was asked.

I love sports, all kinds. I was either credited or blamed for that throughout my presidency. But I never said, well, let's have a fishing setting and the press will be more understanding of the need to relax, etc. I never felt the fishing could be used to a political end. It never occurred to me to get two or three reporters together on this boat and show them how much I enjoy the fishing or go out and make some statement to the country to promote recreation. I suspect that if we had done that, given this particular place, some would have written that this was the elite trying to present something to the American people.

I felt you should do those things for your personal well-being and let the chips fall where they may. For the most part, the press was understanding, that I was on vacation, but there was this pressure of the pack to be adversarial.[42]

CHAPTER FOUR

FISHING AND ESCAPE

That Presidents have taken to fishing in an astonishing fashion seems to me worthy of investigation. I think I have discovered the reason; it is the silent sport. One of the few opportunities given a President for the refreshment of his soul and the clarification of his thoughts by solitude lies through fishing.
                                                                    —*Herbert Hoover*

Presidents have only two moments of personal seclusion—prayer and fishing, and they can't pray all the time.   —*Herbert Hoover*

I don't give a continental damn whether I catch a fish or not.
                                                           —*Franklin D. Roosevelt*

These were the kinds of fishing expeditions Rosalynn and I squeezed into the interstices of a busy presidential life. They were always too brief but especially welcome. For a few hours we enjoyed the solitude we badly needed.
                                                                    —*Jimmy Carter*

It totally clears your mind. It's not just catching the fish; it's the background, the environment, the beauty of it all.   —*George Bush*[1]

It was noon, and Bob Boilard—retired machinist and parttime fishing guide—was drinking coffee in his parlor in Biddeford, Maine. The phone rang. "How are they biting, Bob?" said the voice at the other end. This was not a friend from Kittery or a customer from New Jersey. This was George Bush, the President of the United States, calling from *Air Force One*. The plane was about to land at a Maine air force base, and the First Angler wanted his buddy Boilard to tell him where the fish were.

"Mr. President, I can't tell you anything sitting here in my kitchen," Boilard says.

"Well, then, meet me at Walker Point at three o'clock this afternoon."

"Yes, sir."[2]

Most of us today would think that a presidential vacation is an oxymoron. With the world's agonies evident at a flip of a radio dial or an image on CNN, a president dare not be out of touch for more than a few hours. Today's presidential vacation spots are places that can accommodate satellite dishes, fax machines, modems, communications of the most advanced sort, where as much attention is given to the media's comfort as to the president's. Preparations for vacations mimic those for the Persian Gulf War.

In 1883, however, President Chester A. Arthur could travel seven hundred miles from Washington with just a valet and a Secret Service agent who didn't seem to do very much. In the 1920s Calvin Coolidge could leave Washington for two or three months at a time. And even the activist president Franklin D. Roosevelt could take a six-thousand-mile, three-week cruise to the Galapagos Islands in the days before the Munich crisis in 1938.

Some presidents, like Cleveland and Bush, have fled to the woods or to their vacation homes. Others have fled to official and unofficial presidential retreats like Camp David and Key West. And others have found release through one-time escapes to places from Alaska to Florida and from Panama to Maine.

As Hoover observed, "Fishing seems to be one of the few avenues left to Presidents through which they may escape to their own thoughts, may live in their own imaginings, find relief from the pneumatic hammer of constant personal contacts, and refreshment of mind in rippling water."[3]

Bush, too, found fishing soothing. "It totally, totally clears your mind, even when I was President. In this setting you relax. It's not just catching the fish; it's the background, the environment, the beauty of it all. You can get just mesmerized by the waves and the clear surf. So I get a kick out of not just catching or trying to catch a fish, but from being in this setting."[4]

CHESTER A. ARTHUR SNEAKS ACROSS THE BORDER

Chester A. Arthur was an avid fisherman during much of his life. Indeed, he held an Atlantic salmon record of some fifty pounds on a stretch of the Cascapedia River in Quebec before he became president. Once in the office, however, he was determined to keep his vacations within the United States. One place he escaped to was Alexandria Bay[5] on the St.

President Ulysses S. Grant (in the dark jacket) vacationed at Alexandria Bay, New York, in the summer of 1872. Here, he waits for luncheon to be served. THE ANTIQUE BOAT MUSEUM.

Lawrence River in upper New York State, where he traveled in the fall of 1882. The Thousand Islands were becoming a popular resort area. President Ulysses S. Grant had spent a few days fishing there in 1872, when his most notable performance had been to fall out of a red cedar skiff as it docked at Pullman Island. One witness remembered that "every pocket in the Prince Albert suit was leaking" as the President made his way back to the Pullman estate.[6]

Despite the assassination of President James Garfield a year earlier, an event that had put Arthur in office, the President's only protection was a single Secret Service agent, plus a valet.

Hoping to show that Arthur was not only a machine hack but a sponger on the public trough, *New York Sun* editor Charles Dana sent his crack reporter Julian Ralph to record Arthur's week-long fishing vacation.[7]

President Chester A. Arthur prepares to leave on a fishing outing at Alexandria Bay in 1883. At first worried about staying within U.S. borders, he eventually allowed himself to be taken where the fish were: the far side of the St. Lawrence River in Canada. LIBRARY OF CONGRESS.

Arthur, a widower, seems not to have minded having Ralph or other reporters along. In fact, while the other reporters did very little, Ralph went fishing with the President each day, and sent back daily two-thousand-word dispatches full of chatty detail and devoid of censure.

Throughout the week Arthur read late (though not newspapers or public documents, apparently) and rose late and fished when he felt like it. Ralph observed that each evening he would pass Arthur's open sitting room and see the President and his single protector reading and smoking before a blazing fire. The guides grumbled at one point that he slept so late, "it don't matter when he comes now; there aren't no fish." Ralph reported:

> He seems to be as far removed from news of what is going on throughout the land as he is from the news centers themselves. He has no callers of note, and but few of any sort. He

gets no daily newspaper and . . . he used the telegraph very little. When he is approached upon political topics, he positively
declines to say a word.

When Arthur did come down to fish, it was in comfort and style. The
President fished in the steam yacht *Minnie,* a long, narrow craft with a
closed cabin aft and three fishing skiffs attached to the stern. He carried
not only the heavy trolling rods but also half a dozen bamboo fly rods,
"each slender as a carriage whip," with all the attendant hooks, lines,
equipment, gaffs, nets, and a box with hooks, snells, spoons, scissors, knife,
field lines, even a bottle of silver polish. The picnic hampers groaned with
cutlery, pastries, broiled chicken, chops, cold meats, potatoes, and "appropriate beverages." There were fur robes, cushioned seats, a coffee pot, a
toaster, stew kettles, bait buckets, even a double-barreled shotgun for duck
hunting.

Each day Arthur, dressed in a gray suit and a pearl-colored derby,
would come down to the dock and sally forth for four to eight hours.
Once into the fishing grounds of the day, the President would climb into
one of the fishing skiffs or stay in the *Minnie* and fish from a comfortable
chair. He caught bass, muskellunge, and pickerel by the dozen on minnows, lures, and flies. Although he was famous for his salmon fly-fishing
talents, he was quite happy to catch fish with mere bait. It was so relaxing
that one day he even fell asleep while reading a book, but when a tug
awakened him, Ralph reported, he "played with the fish artistically."

Almost every day, a local photographer named McIntyre pursued the
President "like a man after a consulship." Arthur was patient and obliging,
wanting only to be assured that the man did not include the minnow
bucket in the picture of the renowned fly-fisherman President. Politicians
seeking an audience fared less well. "Whenever one has sent to the hotel to
ask if he could be entertained and could see the President, word has been
received that the President desires privacy," wrote Ralph. Early in the week
Arthur had explicitly ordered the crew to avoid Canadian waters so that he
would not break the precedent that sitting presidents never leave the United
States. But by the end of the week, he was perfectly content to go where
the fish were, which included Queen Victoria's dominion. He even allowed
the irrepressible McIntyre to take pictures of him in a foreign land.

On the last day, Ralph reported that the President's party had caught
nineteen fish in all. The trip ended with Arthur rested and those who had
met him contented.

The only sour note Ralph heard was sounded by the guides who complained that Arthur was a piker on tips and, as one of them moaned, "not as free with his thanks as many of the regular summer boarders. . . . [T]he President is so used to attention that he looks upon the utmost we can do for him as no more than is justly due him."

CLEVELAND ESCAPES TO THE NORTH WOODS AND CAPE COD

Early in his first term, the intense pressure of the job seekers on Grover Cleveland as the first Democratic president in twenty-seven years persuaded him to get clean away from Washington. (The Pendleton Act establishing the civil service had only been passed in 1883.) Together with a few friends from Albany and four experienced guides, Cleveland headed into the Adirondack woods around Saranac Lake. Secretaries, aides, Secret Service—all were left behind on this combination fishing and hunting trip. Cleveland spent most of his days fishing and his evenings playing euchre. The men shared a twenty-seven-by-ten-foot cabin and apparently slept in their clothes on balsam branches spread on the dirt floor. Several nights they even jacked deer, shooting animals temporarily mesmerized in a lantern's beam.

The *New York World* sent a reporter on a two-day tramp to track down the lost President. When he arrived, Cleveland's company greeted him affably. Despite being invited to join their meal, the winded reporter could not hide his censure.

> The President asked me to join them at breakfast and told the cook to "place one more plate." The meal consisted of broiled venison, baked potatoes, hot biscuits, and tea with condensed milk. It was served on a rough board supported on stakes. Large logs were used as chairs. Everything was primitive in the extreme. There was not the slightest thought of form or formality. While we sat at table, I had an excellent opportunity to observe the President's appearance. He seemed even to have gained considerable flesh since he entered the mountains, and his manner betokened some fatigue and lassitude. I was told by one of his guides that the arduous journey through the forest had exhausted him so much that for two days after reaching camp he had been unable to move freely about. Small wonder, speaking from my own experience! The life he is leading in his

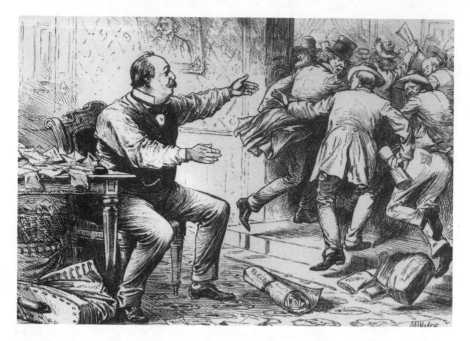

Back from an invigorating fishing trip to the Adirondacks, Grover Cleveland drives off human black flies (job seekers) with a vow to tell them his fish stories. That year he wrote: "This office-seeking is a disease—I am entirely satisfied of that. It is even catching. Men get it, and they lose the proper balance of their minds. I've known men to come here to Washington on other business, with no thought of office, but when they had been here a couple of weeks they had caught it." CORBIS-BETTMANN.

retreat in the wilderness is too much for him. It is totally unadapted for any but the hardiest woodsman.[8]

In the interregnum between his two terms, Grover Cleveland practiced law in New York City. When his wife returned ecstatic from a visit to the area around Buzzards Bay in Massachusetts, Cleveland bluntly asked the host, *Century* magazine editor Richard Gilder, "Are there any fish?" Yes, there were plenty of bluefish and sea bass available in the bay, and trout in nearby streams. After renting cottages on the bay for several years, the Clevelands bought a two-story shingled cottage on several acres of Monument Point next to the home of the actor Joe Jefferson.

For the next decade "Gray Gables" would offer the Clevelands fish, seclusion, and engaging friends, such as Gilder, the publisher William Appleton, the railroad builder John Forbes, and Richard Olney, who would become his attorney general and later secretary of state. It would provide a happy place to raise their children and a welcome retreat from the tensions and pains of Cleveland's second term.

He and Gilder often fished in a small catboat, named after his eldest daughter, Ruth. Or they might go by carriage with the Jeffersons to the Indian village of Mashpee on Cape Cod. Jefferson's son had bought three islets on a small pond there, and there the men fished frequently. They jokingly renamed the three islets Cometoit, Getoffit, and Stayonit.[9]

Cleveland could take his fishing seriously, even grimly. After watching Cleveland fish through the foulest kinds of weather, Gilder wrote, "Grover Cleveland will fish when it shines and fish when it rains; I have seen him pull bass up in a lively thunderstorm, and refuse to be driven from a Cape Cod pond by the worst hailstorm I ever witnessed or suffered. He will fish through hunger and heat, lightning and tempest. . . . This, I have discovered, is the secret of Cleveland luck; it is hard work and no let up."[10]

After Cleveland left the White House, the family continued to spend happy vacations at Gray Gables. Then, family tragedy struck when his beloved daughter Ruth caught diphtheria and died in January 1904. As biographer Allen Nevins wrote, for years Cleveland had worried about the impending Cape Cod canal to be built right past the estate. Now, he and the family also "shrank from the anguish of going back to the familiar scene without Ruth." They sold Gray Gables and bought a new summer home near Tamworth, New Hampshire, where, according to Nevins, he took up fresh-water fishing enthusiastically.[11]

(The house eventually burned and nothing remains on the site. A housing development is on the former estate, with many of the streets named after Cleveland's aides and friends, such as Vilas, Lamont, Jefferson, and Gilder.)

THEODORE ROOSEVELT AND THE RIVER OF DOUBT

In 1913–14 the indefatigable Theodore Roosevelt joined an exploration of a feeder river to the Amazon basin. It wasn't a fishing jaunt or even a hunting expedition so much as an adventure—an adventure that nearly killed the Rough Rider. Its fevers and physical strain broke his health. His book about this trip, *Through the Brazilian Wilderness,* mentions fish and fishing quite frequently, but most of the references relate to fish as food, not to fishing as recreation. In the appendix, Roosevelt outlines the fishing equipment the well-prepared explorer should take.

For small fish like the pacu and the piranha an ordinary bass hook will do. For the latter, because of its sharp teeth, a hook with a long shank and phosphorous-bronze leader is the best; the same character of leader is best on the hook to be used for the big fish. A tarpon hook will hold most of the great fish of the rivers. A light rod and reel would be a convenience in catching the pacu. We used to fish for the latter variety in the quiet pools while allowing the canoe to drift and always saved some of the fish as bait for the big fellows. We fished for the pacu as the native does, kneading a ball of manioc farina with water and packing it on the hook as bait. I should not be surprised, though, if it were possible, with carefully chosen flies, to catch some of the fish that every once in a while we saw rise to the surface to drag some luckless insect under.[12]

As fishing historian Paul Schullery observed drolly, "Roosevelt's Brazilian fishing was done for survival, but he at least recognized a future sporting opportunity. Carefully chosen flies, indeed."[13]

CALVIN COOLIDGE LEARNS TO FISH

Today it is inconceivable that a president could take months of vacation, yet in the summers of 1926, 1927, and 1928, Calvin Coolidge left Washington for stays of six weeks, two months, and almost three months. One of his principal activities was fishing.

Coolidge never said much about his own fishing, but his Secret Service chief Edmund Starling was not so laconic. Himself an avid fly-fisherman, he vowed to convert Coolidge to fishing generally and to fly-fishing especially. It took him three summers but he succeeded.

In the summer of 1926, the Coolidges spent six weeks at Lake Osgood in the northern Adirondacks. There, Coolidge began his fishing apprenticeship under Starling's instruction. (See Chapter Nine.)

For his 1927 summer vacation, Coolidge chose the dry climate of the Black Hills of South Dakota, in part because of Grace Coolidge's respiratory problems. They established camp on the 100,000-acre Custer State Park with an executive office at the Rapid City High School thirty-two miles away, and Coolidge made the hour-long drive several days a week. He did some work, but he was not overly strained. Moreover, the public was far more interested in Charles Lindbergh, who had just flown single-handedly across the Atlantic and was then traveling around the United States.

In the spring of 1927, President Coolidge had the luxury of contemplating a half dozen invitations to fish that next summer. He chose South Dakota's Black Hills. WASHINGTON STAR, *1927. REPRINTED WITH PERMISSION.*

The fishing was excellent, in part because Starling made sure that the streams where Coolidge fished were amply stocked with lochleven and rainbow trout.

This vacation was notable also for the blossoming of Mrs. Coolidge's fishing skill. Accompanied by Secret Service agent James Haley, Grace Coolidge waded through underbrush, carried her own rod, reel, and creel, baited her own hook with worms, and eventually removed her own size-able rainbow trout, which she took home and had cooked for the President's lunch.[14]

Unfortunately, Mrs. Coolidge's fishing was short-lived. According to Starling, one day while the President was at the temporary White House in Rapid City, Agent Haley took Grace Coolidge for a long walk in the hills and, being unused to the woods, got lost. When Coolidge returned, he was incensed. He sent out search parties, who finally met the couple on

*Coolidge shows the day's catch to his wife, Grace, and their dog, Rob Roy, probably in
South Dakota in 1927.* J. R. GREENE AND THE CALVIN COOLIDGE MEMORIAL FOUNDATION.

the path back. Within minutes, Haley was banished from the detail, and
Starling was put in charge of Mrs. Coolidge's security.

"I found myself in a fine fix," wrote Starling. "Mrs. Coolidge could
not go walking unless I went with her. But if the President wanted me to
go fishing, I had to go with him and she had to stay at home."[15]

The following summer, at the suggestion of Wisconsin senator Irvine
L. Lenroot, a competitor for the vice presidential nomination in 1920 and
a friend of the Coolidges, the President accepted an invitation to stay on
the famous Brule River in northern Wisconsin. He had told the world that
he chose "not to run," and his principal concern again seemed to be the
health of his wife. He also chose not to attend the Republican Party's convention and, indeed, was apparently asleep in his railway car on the way to
the Brule when Herbert Hoover won the nomination.

Lenroot had learned that the Henry Clay Pierce estate near Lake Superior was available for rental. Starling visited and gave his imprimatur for the
right mixture of fish, security, and comfort. The encampment covered four
thousand acres, held dozens of lakes connected with canals and locks, and
an eight-room house on an acre-sized island. An eight-foot wire fence surrounded the entire estate, and several look-out towers were already in
place. The estate contained stables, a dairy barn, its own power house, and

The Lure

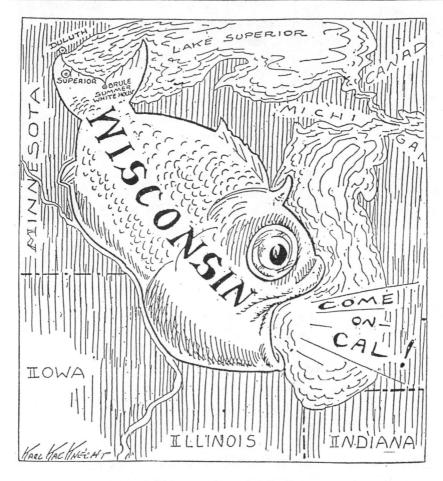

The cartoonist Karl Kae Knecht of the Evansville (Indiana) Courier *imagined the welcome that the people of northern Wisconsin extended to the President in the summer of 1928.* EVANSVILLE COURIER.

a private fish hatchery reputed to be more extensive than any in the state. The Coolidges had a staff of over two hundred to serve and protect them: guards, secretaries, stenographers, a personal physician, eleven Secret Service officers, army and navy aides, six chauffeurs, and twelve household servants, including chief housekeeper, valet, doorman, barber, head cook, butler, and a personal maid to Mrs. Coolidge.[16]

They set up executive offices in the library of Central High School in Superior, about an hour's drive away, installed telephone and telegraph lines and air links with Washington, and the Coolidges settled in for the summer. After ten days of rain, the weather brightened, and starting on Coolidge's birthday, July 4th, the President fished for most of the rest of the summer.

One day reporters asked Coolidge how many fish there were in the river. About 45,000 he estimated. "I haven't caught them all yet," he said, "but I've intimidated them."[17]

HOOVER FLEES TO THE RAPIDAN

Even before the Crash in October 1929, the pressures of the job and the loathsome Washington climate sent Herbert Hoover in search of a retreat. His aides Lawrence Richey and marine colonel Earl Long found a promising location at the headwaters of the Rapidan River in Virginia, about one hundred miles from Washington at a cool elevation of 1,500 feet. The site also offered some trout fishing. Hoover the engineer spent many hours building pools by hand in the stream and then had the waters stocked with rainbows.

Refusing public monies, Hoover himself bought the 164-acre site for $5 per acre and leased another two thousand surrounding acres for protection and riding trails. His wife, Lou Henry, oversaw the construction, from a series of tents to a grouping of rustic beam-buildings, including the President's lodge, or "Brown House," two mess halls, cottages for presidential aides, guest cabins, and a central building called the Town Hall. There was no central heating in the Hoovers' fastidious camp; only dead wood was allowed for cooking and heating. Guests were reminded that they were roughing it, and Lou Henry's advice for cold nights was posted in all guest cottages: "After all blankets and eiders are exhausted, put on your camel's hair dressing gown, wrap your head in a sweater, and throw your fur coat over everything!"[18]

Hoover with his wife stand below the "Brown House" at the presidential retreat they built on the Rapidan River. HOOVER PRESIDENTIAL LIBRARY.

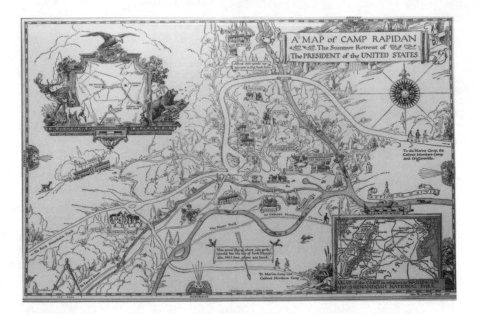

A map done by Mr. William Campbell for a booklet about the Hoovers' Rapidan property. The camp was 2,300 feet high and offered the Hoovers both escape and cool weather. HOOVER PRESIDENTIAL LIBRARY.

Among those guests were Charles and Anne Lindbergh, Winston Churchill, publisher William Allen White, journalist Mark Sullivan, and Thomas Edison.

Hoover even carried out some foreign policy at the Rapidan retreat. In October 1929, according to newspaper accounts, he and British prime minister Ramsay MacDonald sat on a log near the stream and laid the basis for the Disarmament Treaty, which limited the naval strengths of Britain, France, Italy, Japan, and the United States.[19]

According to Secret Service chief Edmund Starling, the river was, alas, plagued with eels that depleted the trout population, requiring frequent restocking. Starling also had a stream-side view of the Great Depression's effect on Hoover's angling. "As the years went by and the Depression came, President Hoover grew nervous. His hands would tremble as he worked with his tackle. I have seen him catch a fishhook in his trousers, his coat, and then in his hat. It was odd to see this, for he looked like a man without a nerve in his body."[20]

Perhaps inevitably, the Rapidan camp became a political issue during the 1932 campaign when Democrats accused Hoover of building the

Escape was certainly not absolute, as Grover Page of the Louisville Courier-Journal *showed in his sympathetic cartoon of the President struggling to tie on a fly in publicity's fishbowl.* LOUISVILLE COURIER-JOURNAL.

*In the early 1950s, cartoonist "Ding" Darling took note of the rabid attention the press
paid to Hoover and Eisenhower when they fished together. In this personal note to
a friend, Darling excoriated the Eisenhower administration's plan to build a dam on the
Upper Colorado River in the Dinosaur National Monument.* COURTESY THE J. N. "DING"
DARLING FOUNDATION.

retreat with government funds and labor (in the form of marine construction units). Hoover, through Secretary of the Navy Charles Francis Adams,
was forced to issue a point-by-point rebuttal that detailed how he had
bought the land at fair market value, how the marines were "on duty"
anyway, and how he had furnished the camp entirely with his own funds.[21]
After his defeat, Hoover deeded the property to the federal government,
and it was incorporated in the Shenandoah National Park. Much later, he
would write:

> When you get full of telephone bells, church bells, office
> boys, columnists, pieces of paper and the household chores—
> you get the urge to go away from here. Going fishing is the
> only explanation in the world that even skeptics will accept.[22]

The skeptics never did leave Hoover in peace—but that had nothing to
do with his fishing and everything to do with his presidential stewardship.[23]

The cartoonist Jay N. Darling visited Hoover on the Rapidan a number of times. In a letter to a friend, Darling described how he and Hoover
had once hidden from the Secret Service.

One day when he and I were out horse back riding in the
Smoky Mountains, we plotted to duck away from the cohort of
bodyguards that usually rode ahead and behind and sneaked off
on a side trail that was hardly visible and rode like hell until we
felt pretty safe. Then we took another side trail and wound up
at an old deserted observation tower of the Forestry Service. We
hitched our horses off in the brush, climbed up into the top of
the tower, and spent the whole day there—cooked our own
lunch, built a dam in a little creek that ran near the tower, caught
a mess of trout for the frying pan, but the most fun was watching
from the top of the tower the secret service men scouring the
countryside to find the President. It is the only time in my life I
ever saw the man really happy and unrestrained.[24]

FDR'S MANY FISHING RETREATS

Fishing became part of Franklin D. Roosevelt's rehabilitation program after
his polio attack. In 1923 he and his Harvard buddy John S. Lawrence of
Boston had purchased a houseboat in Florida. They named the seventy-
one-foot craft the *Larooco,* for "Lawrence-Roosevelt Company." During
the winters of 1924–26, Roosevelt "lost himself from the world almost
completely," according to his son James, using the craft in Florida for a
combination of swimming, fishing, reading, and entertaining.

During the second year's cruise, James reported that "after catching a
thirty-five-pound barracuda, [Father] was through to the deck of the
launch when a heavy squall blew up. 'Had to be passed in through galley
window . . .' he wrote [in the log]. The ligaments of a leg and knee were
torn, and he was immobilized for several days."

Eventually, the expense of the craft and the slowness of his overall
recovery caused Roosevelt and Lawrence to sell the boat for scrap in 1926.[25]

Meanwhile, he had discovered Warm Springs, Georgia, and the thera-
peutic effects its hot water had on his wasted legs. For two years Roosevelt
used its indoor pools and became "Dr. Roosevelt" to dozens of similarly
afflicted people who flocked to the resort. In 1926 he bought the resort
and eventually pumped two-thirds of his fortune into a foundation for
polio treatment. Warm Springs would be a favorite retreat to the end of his
life. There he got the benefit of the baths, but he could also do some fishing for perch in nearby ponds.

Roosevelt fished through the campaign of 1932, and he fished when
he became president—dozens of times. It was almost all salt-water fishing.

FDR with son Elliott and an unidentified crewman on the Larooco *with an immense grouper, either 1924 or 1925.* FRANKLIN D. ROOSEVELT LIBRARY.

Taken at Warm Springs in 1924, this is one of the very rare photos showing FDR with his heavy braces, which were quite painful to wear. Obviously, FDR wanted to fish.
FRANKLIN D. ROOSEVELT LIBRARY.

So often did he fish and so many fish did he bring back to Washington that the waiting room for guests outside Roosevelt's White House office became known as the Fish Room, for all the angling memorabilia kept there.[26]

Depending on whether the President fished in the Atlantic or the Pacific, the Navy was ready with two sets of presidential "cruise gear." Within a day of notification, an elevator would be installed on the vessel, and throughout "Presidential country," as a cruiser would be designated, ramps would be built so that he could move around the deck in his wheelchair. Official business did reach him—daily mail drops, constant radio contact, correspondence. But it didn't require much time. During the daytime Roosevelt did a lot of deep-sea or bottom fishing, and evenings were spent at cocktails, poker, and movies.[27]

Usually the President was accompanied by a fishing launch that would be put out to sea on calm days. Two seats were mounted on the stern.

Most times the President fished, he was accompanied by a member of the party, the captain of the cruiser, and an experienced fisherman among the crew.[28]

Much as he loved to fish, it was never easy for Roosevelt. Secretary of the Interior Harold Ickes described how laborious it was to maneuver the President around the ship and into the fishing boats. About a Roosevelt cruise in 1935, Ickes wrote:

> When the [cruiser] *Houston* anchored, a companionway was lowered from the leeside of the ship and the President's fish launch was brought alongside the little platform at the foot of the companionway. Then two men would carry him sideways down the companionway. They would hand him over to Captain Brown and the other man I have referred to, who would swing him around into his armchair. There he would sit and fish. Especially when the water was rough, as it was sometimes, I was a good deal worried about this transshipment of the President to and from his fishing launch. Any misstep or any sudden lurch of the launch might have caused an accident resulting in serious injury to him. But he never seemed to mind. . . . Cheerfully he submitted to being wheeled up and down the special ramps that had been installed on the *Houston* for his use, or to being carried up and down like a helpless child when he went fishing. He was an avid fisherman and, with his strong arms and shoulders, he was able to give a good account of himself if he once got a fish on his hook. Fortunately, he was a lucky fisherman, also.[29]

During a press conference on the railroad train back to Washington from a Texas fishing trip in May 1937, Roosevelt said somewhat disingenuously,

> The objective of these trips, you know, is not fishing. You have probably discovered that by this time. I don't give a continental damn whether I catch a fish or not. The chief objective is to get a perspective on the scene which I cannot get in Washington any more than any of you boys can. . . . You have to go a long ways off so as to see things in their true perspective; because if you sit in one place, right in the middle of the woods, the little incidents that don't mean a hill of beans get magnified by a president just as they do by a correspondent.[30]

While his ship, the cruiser Indianapolis, *took on fuel at Port-of-Spain, Trinidad, FDR, in the dark shirt, took a few hours off for some dory fishing in the Gulf of Paria.* AP/WIDE WORLD PHOTOS.

In August 1938, Franklin Roosevelt combined business with pleasure by steaming to the Galapagos Islands on the battle cruiser *Houston.* The trip was successful both for the President's angling success and for the specimens collected by the Smithsonian Institution staff led by Dr. Waldo Schmitt. On this three-week trip, members of the presidential and Smithsonian party caught eighty-three different species of fish, including two new species of goboid fish. One of these was named after the President, *Pycnomma roosevelti.*

"Throughout the cruise [FDR] took an active part and a live interest in all our collecting," wrote Schmitt.

Among the fish FDR caught was a twenty-pound rainbow runner and a 230-pound tiger shark, which he fought for an hour and a half. Most interesting was the snaring of a nine-and-a-half foot one-hundred-pound sailfish in the knotted loop of his line. While fighting a larger sailfish, FDR

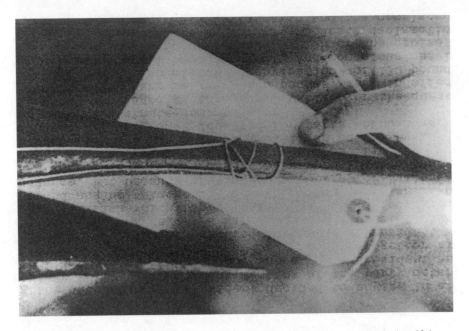

The bill of the sailfish that FDR caught, showing the line from another hooked sailfish wrapped around it. August 1938. FRANKLIN D. ROOSEVELT LIBRARY.

had snared this sailfish by the "beak." Even though the larger fish eventually got away, this fish was brought to gaff.

The President even wrote a foreward to the Smithsonian's account of the expedition, in which he suggested future collaborations between the navy and the Smithsonian. "We cannot know too much about this natural world of ours. We should not be satisfied merely with what we do know. . . ."[31]

Until World War II, Roosevelt did much of his East Coast fishing from aboard the converted Coast Guard ship *Potomac*. This ship weighed 450 tons, was 165 feet long, could steam at 14 knots, and carried a complement of 50 men. A deckhouse was built that contained a lounge, a dining salon, and the President's stateroom. Roosevelt could easily fish from the stern or be transferred to a smaller craft. Other accommodations were made for up to six guests and the Secret Service contingent. In 1940, fifty-caliber machine guns were added fore and aft.

During the war, the *Potomac* was returned to sea duty as a patrol craft and since the Secret Service was not happy to have the President use a craft unprotected against air attack (the machine guns notwithstanding),

In May 1943, Churchill and FDR retreated to Shangri-La to discuss the war and dip a line for fish. As naval aide William Rigdon recalled, "The cigars created enough of a screen to protect both of them from mosquitoes. They would sit there and talk by the hour. . . ." FRANKLIN D. ROOSEVELT LIBRARY.

Roosevelt began to look for another place of regular retreat from Washington's pressures and heat. Discreet enquiries led to a former Civilian Conservation Corps camp in the Catoctin Mountains of Maryland about sixty-five miles west of Washington. According to William Rigdon, one of Roosevelt's aides, the camp proved ideal for the demands of comfort, seclusion, and security. Roosevelt named the camp Shangri-La, after the mythical Himalayan utopia of James Hilton's novel. (The name was kept by President Truman but was changed to Camp David by President Eisenhower.) The camp was guarded by a detachment of marines who lived in an adjacent camp. Next to it was a training camp for Office of Strategic Services (OSS) spies, and Rigdon said one worry was that overly enthusiastic trainees might test their skills by breaking into the President's compound. None did.

Roosevelt liked to fish in the Hunting Creek, which ran through the camp. The national park rangers always stocked the creek with brook trout, although the President was not told of this service. Prime Minister Winston Churchill was a guest at Shangri-La, and on at least two occasions he went with the President to the creek. As Rigdon recalled, "The two men sat side by side on portable canvas chairs—the President pole fishing and Churchill smoking. The cigars created enough of a screen to protect both of them from mosquitoes. They would sit there and talk by the hour. Neither I nor anyone else came close enough to know what they talked about on these informal occasions."[31]

IKE RETREATS TO COLORADO

Dwight Eisenhower went fly-fishing over forty times during his eight years as president, in Georgia, Colorado, Maine, Vermont, Rhode Island, Maryland, and Pennsylvania and even once in Argentina. Even so, fishing was a distant second to golf. The authors of a recent book on presidential golf estimate that Ike played almost eight hundred rounds during his eight years in office.[32]

At a press conference during his second term, Eisenhower observed, "There are three [sports] that I like all for the same reason—golf, fishing, and shooting—because they take you into the fields. . . . They induce you to take at any one time two or three hours, when you are thinking of the bird or the ball or the wily trout. Now, to my mind, it is a very healthful, beneficial kind of thing, and I do it whenever I get a chance."[33]

Early in his first term he visited his brother Milton, who was president of Pennsylvania State College. As soon as the pair stepped outdoors to fish, they were besieged with onlookers and kibitzers. They peppered the President with bits of advice and proffers of angling gadgets to make him more successful. Eisenhower was apparently not amused, and although the pair caught fish, he changed his principal fishing venue to Colorado.

Henceforth, Eisenhower did much of his fishing there, at least until his heart attack in 1955. After that he fished at private clubs in Rhode Island and Connecticut. In Colorado he was usually the guest of his friend, the builder Aksel Nielsen. Byers Peak Ranch was Nielsen's getaway sixty-five miles west of Denver and at an altitude of 8,500 feet. There was plenty of fishing, for three miles of the St. Louis River ran through the ranch. Nielsen had built a cluster of simple cabins, and Ike stayed in the only one that was heated.

According to Alfred Lansing in *Collier's* magazine, Eisenhower fished with a six-foot one-and-a-half-ounce bamboo rod and dry flies. He

A grinning Eisenhower shows off the handsome brown trout he caught at the Hianloland Farms in Rhode Island in 1958. DWIGHT D. EISENHOWER LIBRARY.

carried no creel and put his catch in a grass-lined pocket of his fishing vest. Ike would fish all day but preferred the evening between six and eight, and he dressed in sober clothing, never white. Although he carried a complement of Ginger Quills, Rio Grande Kings, and Red Variants, his favorite fly was the House and Lot, which had been designed by a Denver high school teacher, Ralph Coffman. Nielsen so named the fly because "it gets all over the place—it'll find fish where you'd sworn there never were any."

He and Nielsen or other fishing companions would talk constantly during their fishing, mostly joshing insults. And if he couldn't catch fish on flies, Eisenhower was not above using a spinner, "that last resort thing," but asked the reporters not to "hold this against me."[34]

Knowing of Hoover's love of fishing, Eisenhower once invited the former president to join him in some presumably quiet angling. But the press swarmed around the pair like black flies in June, and they caught few fish. Hoover, who had once observed that only prayer and fishing offered presidents genuine escape from their official duties, remarked to Ike, "I now detect that you have lost the second part."[35]

JIMMY CARTER, FLY-TIER, FLY-SHARER

Calling his conversion to fly-fishing "one of the most gratifying developments of my life," Jimmy Carter later wrote that he looked for chances to pursue it during his presidency. One of those chances was the presidential retreat at Camp David, the "Shangri-La" of FDR.

Richard Nixon took some credit for the Carters' love of Camp David. In his book *In the Arena,* Nixon wrote that in the first year of his presidency, Carter was trying to set an example of parsimony and conservation by cutting back on some presidential perks, such as the yacht and matchbooks and lavish limousines. Included on the hit list was Camp David. Nixon wrote to Carter, urging him to keep the retreat. "The measure of a President's leadership," Nixon wrote further, "is not how many hours he spends at his desk or where his desk is, but how well he makes the great decisions. If getting away from the Oval Office helps him make better decisions, he should get away."[36] Carter took the advice, and as well as a regular refuge for the Carters, Camp David became the site for what was arguably the most important achievement of his presidency, the Camp David Accords between Israel and Egypt. Doubtless, a nearby stream stocked with trout added to the appeal of Camp David as did other trout and bass waters in the vicinity.[37]

One of the Carters' other favorite escapes was Spruce Creek in Pennsylvania, where they stayed with farmer and fisherman Wayne Harpster, who described Carter's approach as follows:

> President Carter was a stickler, and when he decided to do something, he worked at it until he got it done. I think he enjoyed the whole action of going out into the stream and casting and trying to catch fish. It was a good way to clear his mind. And I tried to make it so he could have that kind of therapy.
>
> Dry flies he enjoyed the most by far. Occasionally, when the dry flies weren't doing well, I would try to get him to do nymphs and streamers, and he would sometimes. But he would almost prefer to go out and catch nothing on dry flies to catching fish other ways.

Jimmy Carter nets a fine trout on Spruce Creek at the farm of Wayne Harpster in Pennsylvania. JIMMY CARTER LIBRARY.

> He loved to make flies at Camp David and come down here and fish with them. I'm sure he got more satisfaction out of catching a fish on a fly he tied than any other way.[38]

As Carter's term became wracked with inflation, the Iranian hostage crisis, and soaring energy costs, the President took his fishing escapes wherever he could. In July 1980, on a trip back from Japan, Carter and Secretary of State Edmund Muskie stopped off in Alaska to fish for grayling with Governor Jay Hammond. They flew north from Anchorage to Clarence Lake, near Mt. McKinley. Carter had the satisfaction of not only catching fish but catching them on a fly of his own design. That summer, passage of Alaskan land legislation was a top priority and "this brief trip renewed my determination to succeed, at the same time giving me some new arguments to present to doubtful members of Congress, whose votes I would be seeking back in Washington." Although the trip lasted only six hours, "it was a pleasant respite from the duties of my office, com-

pounded at that time by the Iranian hostage crisis."[39] Even before he left
Alaska, Carter got an earful of citizens' opinions on the bill:

> Later I heard that at the state fair in Fairbanks the Junior
> Chamber of Commerce had accumulated a large pile of empty
> bottles. For a fee the fairgoers could throw them at photographs
> of me, Secretary Andrus, Congressman Mo Udall (a key spon-
> sor of the legislation), and at the Ayatollah Khomeini. I never
> did know for sure who won this "popularity" contest, but I was
> told that my pile of broken bottles was a little larger.[40]

On the morning after Carter lost the election in 1980, he went into
the small office he used as a fishing workshop and carved a small wooden
rack to be used for drying fly line evenly. It was a gift for his Pennsylvania
fishing host and friend, Wayne Harpster.[41]

At the dedication of the International Fly-Fishing Center in West Yellowstone, Montana, in 1981, Jimmy Carter made the following remarks:

> For those who have been in public life, or those who have
> major responsibilities as a mother, or father, or teacher, or a doc-
> tor or an engineer or a farmer like me, you know that there's a
> place where solitude is precious and where companionship with
> friends is equally precious. A place where quiet, undisturbed
> peace is precious and where the most enjoyable excitement of
> catching a big fish, or even losing a big fish, is precious. I'm
> grateful to have a chance to be here for the groundbreaking of
> this fine place, which will mean a lot to fly-fishermen not only
> in our own country but throughout the world. You have blessed
> me by inviting me. I am one of you, and we share a lot in life. I
> hope that when my own time is past, and ours, that we'll leave
> the Earth a little more beautiful and a little purer, and the trout a
> little more ferocious and maybe a little bit larger, than when we
> arrived, not because we didn't catch our share, but because we
> invested for the Amies and the little Sarahs of the world that are
> coming along behind us.
>
> I was pleased as President to have a chance to make some
> momentous decisions. One of the most exciting days of my life
> was when Cecil Andrus, a neighboring governor of yours, as
> secretary of the Interior, and I were able to save with one stroke
> of the pen a hundred million acres of wilderness area in Alaska.

Victor in the 1988 election, George Bush seems to throw himself into his surf fishing in Florida that December. BUSH PRESIDENTIAL LIBRARY.

This is the kind of thing that is gratifying to a president, but to be on a solitary stream with good friends, with a fly rod in your hand, and to have a successful or even an unsuccessful day—they're all successful—is an even greater delight. . . .[42]

BUSH ESCAPES—INTO THE GLEAM OF PUBLICITY

George Bush has fished all his life for all kinds of fish. He fished for mackerel, bluefish, kingfish, barracuda, sailfish, bonefish, bass, and trout. He fished in Wyoming, Idaho, Alaska, Florida, Alabama, and Texas, but his favorite spot was the family place at Walker Point in Kennebunkport, Maine. Most of us would hardly call it an escape to be surrounded by the Secret Service, electrified fences, protective shrubbery, and the Coast Guard. But Bush seemed not to mind. After all, he was there before the tourists. He had fished there all his life.

For Bush, fishing's appeal lay in its cleansing quality. "It totally, totally clears your mind. You relax. It's not just catching the fish; it's the background, the environment, the beauty of it all. You can get just mesmerized by these waves and this clear surf. So I get a kick out of not just catching or trying to catch a fish but from being in this setting. . . . I can think about nothing or if I do want to think about certain things, it's a good way to do it. It's not just an escape; it's a good way to concentrate if you want to. It's that combination of the tranquility, the natural beauty, and the chance to escape or concentrate if you want. It's conducive to either relaxing or concentrating."[43]

After he left the White House, George Bush had an experience in which his escape was due to the Secret Service. He had gone to Labrador to fish for salmon.

> We were trying to get into our fishing lodge, and the helicopters had to land because of the weather. I went out to survey the ground, and when I was walking back to the helicopter, I stepped on a patch of ground with only a little moisture on it. Well, I stepped on this mossy place, and I sank into a bog up to my waist. Literally I couldn't move. If I had been alone, I could have been dead.
>
> Fortunately, there was a Secret Service guy and a Royal Canadian Mounted Policeman who pulled and pulled on my arms and out I came, with what Ross Perot would call a giant sucking sound.[44]

CHAPTER FIVE

FISHING, POLITICS, AND THE CARTOONIST'S PEN[1]

The pen is mightier than the politician.   —*Gerald Ford*[2]

A cartoonist may only play upon and reflect the things and emotions that are already before the public. The cartoon is essentially a spotlight service. [The cartoonist] must be content to play his calcium ray upon the marionettes that strut the visible stage.   —*J. N. "Ding" Darling*[3]

In August 1941, with the Nazi invasion of Russia two months old and the war coming closer and closer to American shores, Franklin D. Roosevelt and Winston Churchill arranged to meet secretly in the North Atlantic.

First, FDR told the Press Association in Washington that he meant to get away on the USS *Potomac* for some time off the coast of Maine, and he couldn't take them. Then, after traveling northward by train, the President's party stopped at New London, Connecticut, to board the *Potomac*. The next day he went fishing prominently in the harbor of Nonquit, Massachusetts. That evening, the *Potomac* anchored in the middle of a small flotilla of warships including the USS *Augusta*. In the darkness, the President was transferred to the *Augusta,* and the flotilla headed north for Newfoundland and the rendezvous with Churchill. Meanwhile, Admiral William Leahy had dressed several of his men in civilian clothes and the next day had them lounge around the deck of the *Potomac,* pretending to be the President and his fishing party. Later in the day, the *Potomac* weighed anchor and proceeded up the coast.

By the end of that day the press (and the public) became first curious and then nervous about the President's whereabouts. When Roosevelt didn't show himself, speculation grew that he was on some secret mission.

On August 5, 1941, Vincent Svoboda of the Brooklyn Eagle took Roosevelt's fishing story at face value and imagines the President besieged by paperwork with only an overworked secretary and his dog, Fala, for company. BROOKLYN PUBLIC LIBRARY COLLECTION.

David Low's cartoon has the leaders confidently preparing hook and line for "the big one that won't get away." EVENING STANDARD/SOLO.

Four or five days later, with Churchill safely home in London and Roosevelt back in Washington, the two leaders announced their joint Atlantic Charter, whose proclaimed freedoms and rights would eventually become part of the United Nations Charter.[4]

When editorial cartoonists around the country came to comment upon the historic meeting off Newfoundland, one of the more common images was that of fishing, both because of the angling subterfuge and because FDR's fishing proclivity was well-known to the cartoonists and the public. Word had also leaked out that FDR had done some fishing in Newfoundland while he waited for Churchill. Of these cartoons, only Darling's showed fishermen and catch in a plausible perspective. (Interestingly, the cartoonists give no indication of Roosevelt's polio. That he could not stand unaided, let alone stride with an armload of fish, was not even hinted at.)

Throughout American history cartoonists have chided, derided, mocked, and ridiculed the powerful and the pretentious. They didn't just

THE CATCH.   By Rube Goldberg.

Rube Goldberg has FDR hauling home a load of fish. RUBE GOLDBERG. PROPERTY OF RUBE GOLDBERG INC. DISTRIBUTED BY UNITED MEDIA.

Darling compares the Atlantic Charter to a fish the size of a tuna or shark, August 15, 1941. COURTESY THE J. N. "DING" DARLING FOUNDATION.

The Missing Boys Are Safe And Sound

Richard Yardley portrayed the American and British public's delight at the reform of Roosevelt and Churchill from their "fishing trip" in the North Atlantic. RICHARD YARDLEY, *BALTIMORE SUN;* AUGUST 18, 1941.

nudge their subjects; like the nineteenth century cartoonist Thomas Nast, they tried to "hit the enemy between the eyes and knock him down." A balanced view was failure.

To do this they called upon all available images. Nothing was out of bounds to the cartoonist. As Stephen Hess and Milton Kaplan have written: "[B]asically political cartooning is a symbolic art. The symbols are a shorthand, a convenience, not only for the artist but for the viewer as well. . . . [The] materials from which cartoonists mined their political similes and metaphors were determined by their own interests and education and those of their audiences."[5] Had Roosevelt not been such a well-known fisherman, or had his mysterious trip not begun with some fishing, far fewer cartoonists would have reached for those angling images.

In addition, political cartooning has always been a hasty art. Cartoonists are not drawing for the ages, but for the morning or afternoon subscriber. Their images have to "read." In any one cartoon, the catch might be a piece of legislation, an electoral victory, an idea, a convert. Thus were campaigns, policies, and people transformed into bait, equipment, fish caught, and fish lost. It's worth noting that very few of the images dealt with presidential recreation per se. (Fred Seibel's swipe at Franklin Roosevelt's fishing was an exception. See p. 199.)

The cartoon might be artistic but it was above all a medium for conveying ideas. As Florence Berryman, the daughter of long-time *Washington Star* cartoonist Clifford Berryman, wrote, "A drawing may be beautifully executed, may have decorative qualities, admirable composition, and creative design, all of which make it good art. But unless it presents an idea forcefully and convincingly, it is not a good cartoon."[6]

In the Basil O'Connor collection of political cartoons at the Roosevelt Library in Hyde Park, New York, there are hundreds of images of FDR fishing.[7]

By no means, however, was Roosevelt the only presidential angler who appeared in political cartoons. The use of fishing images goes back at least to the 1880s. In the first of three nineteenth century cartoons that follow, Uncle Sam (with Washington holding the net) angles for a Republican nominee at the Chicago convention in 1884. Rising to the bait or just coming up for air are such figures as President Chester A. Arthur, Ulysses S. Grant, Benjamin Butler, Benjamin Harrison, Roscoe Conkling, and the eventual nominee, James Blaine, who would lose to Democrat Grover Cleveland. The second cartoon (from 1892) shows Cleveland's return from

George Washington fishing with Uncle Sam in the Republican pool for an 1884 presidential candidate. COURTESY THE LIBRARY OF CONGRESS.

Cleveland with Harrison—1892. LIBRARY OF CONGRESS.

1888 Decker cartoon on Grover Cleveland. BENJAMIN HARRISON HOME.

the wilderness, where Benjamin Harrison had dispatched him in 1888, to defeat Harrison for a second term—and claim the presidential fish.

The third image is from a series of Republican attacks on Cleveland from an album presented to Benjamin Harrison "with best wishes of J. C. Decker, Special Cartoonist N.Y.C. & Co. Coni, Campaign 1888." The bait Cleveland hangs out reads For A Second Term. And the sign throws Cleveland's own words back at him: "Public Office is a Public Trust." Will the Public Trust Me Again? Echo Answers No!

The Democrats were hard-pressed to find a candidate to run against the energetic Theodore Roosevelt in 1904. The name of Grover Cleveland, now retired to Princeton, was bandied around. In the first cartoon, the cartoonist has the Democrats trying to awaken presidential ambitions in the sleeping angler, Cleveland, while an irritated William Jennings Bryan looks on. In the second, cartoonist Clifford Berryman implies that a 1903 Cleveland trip west is really a campaign warm-up. Roosevelt trounced the ultimate Democratic nominee, Alton B. Parker of New York, 56 percent to 38 percent, with Socialist Eugene Debs winning 3 percent.

Because William Howard Taft did *some* fishing, *Washington Star* cartoonist Clifford Berryman used this device in an image from the pivotal election of 1912. In it, when Theodore Roosevelt, incensed at the conservative trend in the Republican Party, ran against his chosen successor, his

WILL HE BITE?

Cleveland the angler asleep in 1903. COURTESY THE LIBRARY OF CONGRESS.

convention delegate total was puny. He then bolted the Republicans to establish the Progressive Party.

Berryman again called on the fishing device after the election of 1920 to show how Republican Warren G. Harding foiled Democrat James M. Cox. Harding's handlers argued that the less he said and did, the better. They adopted what had been known as the "front porch strategy" in William McKinley's day. Harding stayed home in Marion, Ohio, and received delegations with platitudinous remarks, while Cox and his running mate, Franklin D. Roosevelt, barnstormed the country giving hundreds of speeches. Harding won.

Harding lost no time in getting away for a golf and fishing vacation in Texas. Berryman drew the President-elect with his equipment.

Berryman on Cleveland's western trip in 1903. WASHINGTON STAR, 1903. REPRINTED WITH PER-
MISSION.

Berryman on TR and Taft in 1912. WASHINGTON STAR, 1912. REPRINTED WITH PERMISSION.

*Berryman on Harding and Cox in 1920. WASHINGTON STAR, 1920. REPRINTED WITH
PERMISSION.*

When Calvin Coolidge vacationed in the Adirondacks in 1926, *Des
Moines Register* cartoonist J. N. "Ding" Darling deftly posed the dilemma of
a fishing President: how to balance the demands of the job and the fish.
Coolidge's fishing enthusiasm was a product of Secret Service chief
Edmund Starling's tutelage. In this image, the caption read, Wanted: More
Information. What Does The President Do Under Such Circumstances?

By May 1927, the press and public knew that Coolidge was headed for
a South Dakota vacation in the Black Hills. In anticipation of some more
presidential angling, cartoonist Clifford Berryman penned a drawing to
show that Coolidge would still have to deal with some thorny issues, such
as Prohibition. The woman-in-waiting is Miss Democracy, a stock character Berryman employed to represent the People.

Darling on Coolidge in the Adirondacks. COURTESY THE J. N. "DING" DARLING FOUNDATION.

Berryman on Coolidge and Prohibition. WASHINGTON STAR, 1927. REPRINTED WITH PERMISSION.

When Coolidge finally did arrive in the Black Hills in June 1927, with his legions of aides, protectors, and press people, Ding Darling contrasted that July Fourth–like parade with the barefoot-boy-and-his-can-of-worms approach any ordinary or sensible person would, of course, use.

In August 1928, Berryman used Coolidge's now-famous announcement of "I choose not to run" as a whimsical way to say Coolidge was happier fishing than being president.

Shortly after the end of World War I, Ding Darling went to see Herbert Hoover to sketch him in person. Darling's fellow Iowan had just returned from his relief work in Europe, and his stock was rising in the Republican Party. Darling wanted a firsthand look at a cartoonist's curse; Hoover's "most average-looking face." Darling did his work and struck up a friendship with Hoover that would last for over forty years. One hobby the two men shared was fishing.

Darling on Coolidge in the Black Hills in 1927. COURTESY THE J. N. "DING" DARLING FOUNDATION.

Coolidge chooses "not to run" in this Berryman cartoon. WASHINGTON STAR, 1928. REPRINTED
WITH PERMISSION.

In 1929, just before the Crash, Darling made a composite drawing of
Hoover's face, traits, and real and imaginary activities. Because Hoover was
well-known as an angler, an image of the "common man" was included.

The next year Darling would show Hoover escaping from the cares of
the office, the growing Depression, and an increasingly fractious Senate.
This cartoon appeared in a collection of Darling cartoons of Hoover.
Under the date February 13, 1930, were some shorthand notes to illumine
the appeal of fishing:

"Frazzled-nerved" senators were delaying tariff action . . .
Senator Borah condemned Hoover's selection of Charles Evan
Hughes as Chief Justice . . . Five-power naval conference failed
to abolish submarine warfare . . . Agricultural papers demanded
the United States withdraw from the Philippines . . . GOP chief

Darling on "Why Presidents Go Fishing." COURTESY THE J. N. "DING" DARLING FOUNDATION.

Berryman on Hoover and department heads. WASHINGTON STAR, 1930. REPRINTED WITH
PERMISSION.

the United States withdraw from the Philippines . . . GOP chief
quizzed on Muscle Shoals lobbying . . .[8]

Clifford Berryman, meanwhile, would portray the harried presidential
angler Hoover as sending his department chiefs out to bring in all possible
good news ("Big Ones") for the collapsing economy.

During the first two weeks of May 1937, when FDR went tarpon
fishing in Texas, over fifty of the cartoons in the O'Connor collection
showed Roosevelt fishing. A few were amiable snapshots of the angling
President. But the great majority dealt with the burning issues of the day
and expressed most emotions from generous approval to venomous scorn.

One cartoon castigated him for the weakness of the Neutrality Law,
which snared tiny Spain but had no effect on the behavior of the European
dictatorships. Another pointed out that even though he was on vacation,
Roosevelt was still hooked to the big fish of deficit spending. A Darling

Doute on Neutrality. JERRY DOUTE IN THE *CAMDEN COURIER-POST.*

HE GENERALLY USES MORE

Darling on federal largesse. COURTESY THE J. N. "DING" DARLING FOUNDATION.

Here Comes the Boss Man

Seibel on court packing, September 28, 1937. FRED O. SEIBEL PAPERS, SPECIAL COLLECTIONS
DEPARTMENT, UNIVERSITY OF VIRGINIA LIBRARY.

Darling on court packing. COURTESY THE J. N. "DING" DARLING FOUNDATION.

Jim Berryman on Churchill and FDR at the Quebec conference. WASHINGTON STAR, 1943.
REPRINTED WITH PERMISSION.

cartoon showed him baiting Congress with billions of dollars of federal largesse.

The greatest uproar in FDR's second term arose from his attempt to pack the Supreme Court with six more (and presumably more sympathetic) justices. Many cartoonists used the fishing image to lambast the President for this assault on the Constitution.

When Clifford Berryman collapsed in 1935, his son Jim took over the cartooning duties at the *Washington Star* and continued there for another thirty years. His style and outlook were akin to his father's and he, too, would use a fishing metaphor on occasion. In the cartoon above, Berryman took note of the fall of Mussolini in Italy in 1943, which occurred

Ike and Hagerty by Berryman. WASHINGTON STAR, 1952. REPRINTED WITH PERMISSION.

when FDR was on a fishing vacation to Canada. The cartoon above shows a wary Dwight Eisenhower listening to press secretary James Hagerty tell him about a 1952 campaign salvo from Harry Truman on behalf of Democratic candidate Adlai Stevenson.

Jimmy Carter's fishing offered an occasional metaphorical device for the cartoonists' jibes. In this case, Carter and Rosalynn had recently been fishing on the Green River in Idaho, and his love of angling was quickly established in the public mind. Here, the *Washington Post's* Herblock in 1978 contrasted the handsome fish Carter caught—the Panama Canal treaty—with his energy bill, which had been picked clean by lobbyists and Congress.

TROPHY ROOM

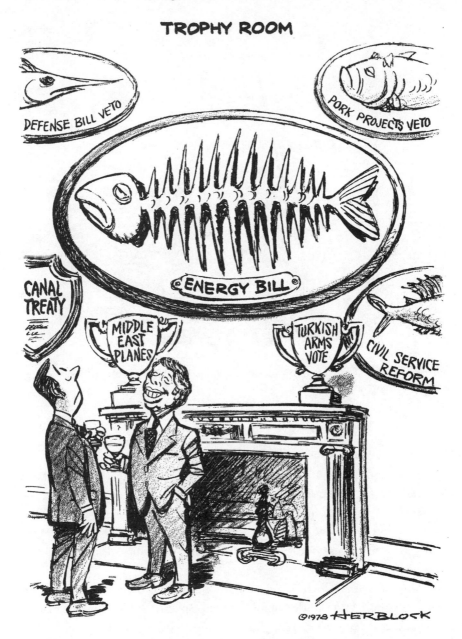

Carter by Herblock. COPYRIGHT 1978 BY HERBLOCK IN THE *WASHINGTON POST.*

"Hooked but still a long way off" by Seibel. FRED O. SEIBEL PAPERS, SPECIAL COLLECTIONS
DEPARTMENT, UNIVERSITY OF VIRGINIA LIBRARY.

From a fisherman's point of view, Fred Seibel was arguably the greatest
political cartoonist in American history. For almost thirty years he drew a
daily cartoon for the *Richmond Times-Dispatch*—more than 13,000 in all—
and scores of them contained a fishing motif. Perhaps this was because
Seibel was himself an avid fisherman. Often he would note the opening or
closing of a fishing season by putting himself (and his "dingbat" Moses
Crow) in a drawing.[9]

Some of Seibel's cartoons were drawn with decidedly more accuracy
than others, reflecting both overall style and specific knowledge of fishing
habits and gear. But even an angler-cartoonist could forget himself, as, in
the cartoon above, when Seibel put the handle on the wrong side of the
reel. The idea was always more important than the metaphor, and few in
the cartoonists' fraternity ever let accuracy besmirch a good image. "I
think every cartoon should do at least one of three things," Seibel once
said. "It should make the reader laugh or cry or think. I usually try to
make him laugh whether I can make him think or not."[10]

"Letting the Boys Have a Little Fun" by Seibel. FRED O. SEIBEL PAPERS, SPECIAL COLLECTIONS
DEPARTMENT, UNIVERSITY OF VIRGINIA LIBRARY.

"Could FDR Land Him if He Tried?" by Seibel. FRED O. SEIBEL PAPERS, SPECIAL COLLECTIONS DEPARTMENT, UNIVERSITY OF VIRGINIA LIBRARY.

"If Eisenhower can go fishin', so can I!" by Seibel. FRED O. SEIBEL PAPERS, SPECIAL COLLECTIONS DEPARTMENT, UNIVERSITY OF VIRGINIA LIBRARY.

CHAPTER SIX

STREAMSIDE SITUATION ETHICS

Lord, suffer me to catch a fish so large that even in talking of it afterward I shall have no need to lie.   *—Anonymous motto for Hoover's fishing lodge*

In essentials—truthfulness; in nonessentials—reciprocal latitude.[1]
                          —Grover Cleveland

An answer to this question
Is what I greatly wish
Does fishing make men liars
Or do only liars fish?

                                             —Anonymous[2]

A fter the press reported on one of Franklin D. Roosevelt's fishing vacations during his first term, the comptroller general of Georgia, W. B. Harrison, wrote to the chief executive:

Dear Mr. President:

Down here in your adopted home nearly all of us are lovers of that greatest of outdoor sports—fishing. In our little group in this department, a great deal of attention was attracted by news stories of your recent wonderful fishing trip, and reminiscent recitation thereon. We are particularly impressed with the attached illustration in which you are showing the measurement of one of your catches on your trip.

Among us in Georgia there is a very exclusive organization to which the membership entitlement is a certain form of license. Attached also herewith is a duly certified copy of the requisite license and the hope that we may count you a highly prized honorary member.

Clifford Berryman shows his skepticism of Roosevelt's court-packing plan in 1937 by adding the same fisherman's prayer that Hoover had put on the wall of his fishing camp.
WASHINGTON STAR, 1937. REPRINTED WITH PERMISSION.

With assurances of the highest regards and sympathetic affection of our group, I beg to subscribe myself, etc.

Attached to this letter was a form from "The Georgia Branch of the Ancient, Reckless and Independent Order of Prevaricators." Across the outline of a fish was written: Fish Liar's License. This is to certify that Franklin D. Roosevelt is entitled to Lie from the 1st day of January to the 31st day of December, he being a duly qualified Liar and [having] satisfied the G.B.A.R. & I.O. of P., that he is a fit and proper person to hold a license. April 12, 1934.

Harrison's letter was no isolated invitation. Roosevelt received memberships in at least four different fishing liars' clubs, and similar licenses were sent to Hoover, Truman, and Eisenhower. More than a score of angler-voters sent Roosevelt copies of the Heddon Liar's License For Fishermen. A man from Coral Gables, Florida, wrote to Roosevelt in October 1934:

Dear President:

Hearing of your fishing exploits, I think it best to insure you from all trouble. But down here is where the big fishes are landed. With best wishes as o'er the miles I send my appreciation, gratitude and my esteem, [signed]

The bearer (The Honorable F.D. Roosevelt), having, by reputation and long practice, coupled with a vivid imagination, exhibited all of the proper requirements therefor, is hereby empowered to Lie, Prevaricate, and show every other recklessness with the Truth, considered expedient by him, in connection with all matters relative to Fish and Fishing, for the current season, subject however to the regulations on the back hereof, In witness hereof is attached the Grand Seal of Ananias, Prince of Liars.

The reverse side listed the regulations and restrictions for such lying:

1. Lies my be told at any place or time without notice. (Note: Not advisable to Game Wardens.)
2. Cameras may be used, scales doctored, and elastic rules employed.
3. Borrowed or rented fish may be used at all times.
4. Guides or others may be bribed or otherwise induced to corroborate all good lies.
5. No lies may be retracted, but may be added to, at will.
6. An extra quarter pound or half inch will improve all lies.
7. This license is null and void if used for any other purpose, including:
a. Weight of babies
b. Tire and gasoline mileage
c. Golf scores
d. Prohibition matters
e. All private or business purposes

Ever since Jonah escaped from the whale, fishing has spawned boasting, exaggeration, and downright falsehood. The tug on the line became a jerk. The dimple on the water became a splash. The perch was magically transformed into a bass, and the lost fish evolved into a lunker.

To George Bush, "lying goes with the territory of fishing. Everyone understands that. We get a striper on here and if you don't bring it in, it's a

INSTRUCTIONS: All Cheerful Liars should be licensed. Use your own judgment.

Liar's License for Fishermen

Issued by Heddon-Dowagiac Dealers and Boosters

THE BEARER _The Honorable F.D. Roosevelt_ having, by reputation and long practice, coupled with a vivid imagination, exhibited all of the proper requirements therefor, is hereby empowered to Lie, Prevaricate, and show every other recklessness with the Truth, considered expedient by him, in connection with all matters relative to Fish and Fishing, for the current Season, subject however to the regulations on the back hereof.

IN WITNESS HEREOF is attached the Grand Seal of Ananias, Prince of Liars.

Signed: _Willie Puff_ (?)

Grand Muskellunge and Heddon Booster

Seal of Ananias
Prince of Liars

"I lie cheerfully"

Exalted Fish Herder and Heddon Tackler

Countersigned

Read the regulations on the other side

O. H. JOHNSON
513 AVENUE SAN LORENZO
CORAL GABLES, FLA.
EVERGREEN 342 J

Copy of the Heddon Liar's License, which was sent to President Franklin Roosevelt at least half a dozen times during his presidency. This one was a gift of a gentleman from Coral Gables, Florida, on learning of the skepticism that greeted FDR's catch in September 1933. FRANKLIN D. ROOSEVELT LIBRARY.

huge fish. It's like the Navy. With every passing year you become more heroic. I've read accounts of my military service [that] I don't recognize it sounds so good."[3]

To most anglers this practice was a harmless part of the chase. Indeed, such streamside situation ethics have been further refined in the last ten to fifteen years. Under the banner of catch and release, a whole new generation of liars has been spawned. They have explained away their empty creels by claiming, for example, that they would only keep trophy fish or that a trout is too precious a fish to be caught only once.

When the fisherman is also a politician, his credibility is even further strained.

Grover Cleveland confronted the problem of fishing and lying head-on. In his delightful *Fishing and Shooting Sketches,* Cleveland ruminated upon the wonders and peculiarities of angling, and particularly the states of mind it induced in its practitioners. Fishing required its own particular species of truth:

> It is sometimes said that there is such a close relationship between mendacity and fishing that in matters connected with their craft, all fishermen are untruthful. It must, of course, be admitted that large stories of fishing adventure are sometimes told by fishermen—and why should this not be? Beyond all question there is no sphere of human activity so full of strange and wonderful incidents as theirs. Fish are constantly doing the most mysterious and startling things; and no one has yet been wise enough to explain their ways or account for their conduct. The best fishermen do not attempt it; they move and strive in the atmosphere of mystery and uncertainty, constantly aiming to reach results without a clue, and through the cultivation of faculties, nonexistent or inoperative in the common mind.[4]

The problem, Cleveland suggested, was not that of the angler but of the listeners and resulted from the lack of suitable preparation by the latter. If they cannot accept a fisherman's story, "it is because their believing apparatus has not been properly regulated and stimulated."

Cleveland continued by spinning out every fisherman's dream—an irresistible explanation for why the biggest one always got away.[5]

> It is constantly said that [fishermen] greatly exaggerate the size of the fish lost. This accusation, though most frequently

and flippantly made, is in point of fact based upon the most absurd arrogance and a love of slanderous assertion that passes understanding. These are harsh words; but they are abundantly justified.

In the first place, all the presumptions are with the fisherman's contention. It is perfectly plain that large fish are more apt to escape than small ones. Of course their weight and activity, combined with the increased trickiness and resourcefulness of age and experience, greatly increase their ability to tear out the hook, and enhance the danger that their antics will expose a fatal weakness in hook, leader, line, or rod. Another presumption, which must be regretfully mentioned, arises from the fact that in many cases the encounter with a large fish causes such excitement on the part of the fisherman as leads him to do the wrong thing or fail to do the right thing at the critical instant— thus actually and effectively contributing to an escape [that] could not and would not have occurred except in favor of a large fish.

Beyond these presumptions we have the deliberate and simple story of the fisherman himself, giving with the utmost sincerity all the details of his misfortune, and indicating the length of the fish he has lost, and given in pounds his exact weight. Now, why should this statement be discredited? It is made by one who struggled with the escaped fish. Perhaps he saw it. This, however, is not important, for he certainly felt it on his rod, and he knows precisely how his rod behaves in the emergency of every conceivable strain.[6]

There you have it: The biggest is the wiliest; the fisherman gets too excited fighting the biggest fish; who knows better than the fisherman himself that the escapee was the biggest fish? The distance from the Biggest Fish to the Big Lie is only a short cast.

For Cleveland and the angling brotherhood, the Golden Rule was: Believe as we would be believed.

An attempt has been made to remedy the indefiniteness of this requirement by insisting that no statement should be regarded as sufficiently truthful for the fisherman's code that had not for its foundation at least a belief of its correctness on the part of the member making it. This was regarded as too much elasticity in the quality of the belief required. The matter seems to have been finally adjusted in a matter expressed in the motto: In essentials—truthfulness; in non-essentials—reciprocal latitude. If it is objected that there may be great difficulty and perplexity in determining what are essentials and what non-essentials under this rule, it should be remembered that no human arrangements, especially those involving morals and ethics, can be made to fit all emergencies.[7]

Cleveland gave an example of excessive "reciprocal latitude" when he addressed a gathering of the Old Colony Club's annual dinner and clambake on Buzzards Bay, Massachusetts.

> You have all heard of a recent event in my family [the birth of his son]. Dr. Bryant officiated as he has always done on such occasions, and after weighing the baby on the same scales [that] he used on our fishing trips together, he announced that the baby weighed sixteen pounds. I did not question this report, although at the time it did seem a trifle heavy. The next morning, still thinking the weight a trifle excessive, I tried the baby on my own scales and found he weighed eight pounds.
>
> Now, I have fished with Dr. Bryant for many years; we have been warm friends, and I have never baited a hook behind his back; *yet he has been weighing his fish all these years on scales which registered a sixteen-pound new-born baby!*[8]

On a 1927 fishing trip in the Black Hills of South Dakota, Calvin Coolidge acknowledged the eternal problem of public skepticism about a fisherman's take. After catching seven trout, he displayed the fish because, as the *New York Times* reported, "scarcely anyone believes a fisherman and [the President] therefore thinks it is wisest to produce the actual evidence."[9]

Coolidge may have been thinking of Cleveland's observations the next year when he was fishing in Yellowstone Park. Wally Eagle, whose family has owned an outfitting store in West Yellowstone, Montana, for over eighty years, recalled:

> Coolidge had been on vacation in 1928. He had come to Yellowstone to fish but also to give a speech in the park. When

Calvin Coolidge acknowledged that the congruence of fishing and lying was such that if you were to be believed, you had to display your catch. AP/WIDE WORLD PHOTOS.

he fished anywhere, I suppose the staff usually blocked off a portion of the stream so that he could fish undisturbed.

On this occasion, he was to fish a stretch of the Fire Hole (which runs down from Old Faithful to connect with the Gibbon River to form Madison). My father, Sam Eagle, had fished that area since 1902 and he knew the park rangers well enough so that they let him and my brother fish in the restricted area that day.

Dad caught a nice mess of fish, and my brother caught one. When they saw the President's party, Dad asked one of the guides if Coolidge had had any luck. "No," said the chagrined guide. Dad asked if he would like to have some of his fish transferred to the President's creel, which the guide was carrying. Indeed he would, the guide said.

Later in the day, after Coolidge had given his speech, he was asked how he had done fishing.

"Well," said the President, "I have always heard that they judge a fisherman's success by the contents of his creel." Then he showed the audience the creel and the fish, which my dad and brother had caught.

No one ever asked Coolidge if he had caught the fish, so he didn't have to choose between lying and the truth.[10]

Other than pin up the quote about lying at his Rapidan camp, Herbert Hoover said little about lying per se. He did observe that anglers gain in "charity when [they] listen to other fishermen."[11]

Fishing also built character, Hoover thought. "Lots of people committed crimes during the year who would not have done so if they had been fishing. The increase of crime is among those deprived of the regenerations that impregnate the mind and character of fishermen."[12]

Franklin D. Roosevelt suffered the indignity of being accused of lying by his own son. In 1934 Roosevelt went on a fishing cruise on Vincent Astor's yacht, the *Nourmahal*. According to his son James, son Elliott was in the doghouse for "some of his exploits which had been in the newspapers."

Father told Vincent [Astor], "Do not let him come aboard!" and went off fishing in a small boat so he would not be there to receive him.

When the [sea]plane [carrying Elliott] landed, it became apparent Elliott had a third strike against him—he had been celebrating the night before and was nursing a monumental hangover. Vincent was in a dilemma: he was loath to disobey the President, but he just couldn't leave Elliott to swelter in the bouncing seaplane anchored off the yacht. He took Elliott aboard and hustled him into a shower.

When Pa returned, he was exceedingly annoyed that his instructions had been disobeyed. "He is to go back with the plane and he is not to have lunch with us!" Father told Vincent. He sent for Elliott and read him a lecture in a voice that carried through the thick doors and walls of his cabin. Then Elliott was sent back on the amphibian.

If the irrepressible Elliott felt disgraced, he certainly did not show it. On landing, he hunted up the newspaper correspon-

*On board Vincent Astor's yacht in April 1934, FDR patiently explains his luck to
newspaper reporters. It was all to refute his son Elliott's statement that the President was
not catching any fish. The President read from various memoranda of various exploits of
the other members of the party and suggests the size of one of their catches. Roosevelt even
went so far as to assert that he had hooked and landed a sperm whale with a three-ounce
rod.* AP/WIDE WORLD PHOTOS.

dents, who were unhappily sequestered in a temporary White
House headquarters at Miami, and told them a fantastic yarn
about the results of a fishing contest in which "Pa's luck was not
so good." The correspondents "demanded" that they be
allowed to visit the *Nourmahal* as an "investigating committee"
to probe these rumors. Pa's anger, as usual, had blown over as
quickly as it had flared; furthermore, he was rather amused by
the manner in which Elliott had carried off the situation. He
sent word that the correspondents might come aboard—I was
their escort—but that Elliott was to remain ashore. A mock trial
was held, with Pa as the "plaintiff" and Elliott as the "absent
defendant," accused of "gross libel." Pa spun a series of diverting
stories, including one about how he had taken a sperm whale

with a three-ounce hook. The trial was "inconclusive," but everyone went back to Miami in good humor.[13]

Mr. Carl Rosenberg, owner of Rosie's Cafe in Miltown, Wisconsin, noted Roosevelt's dilemma and offered the President some comfort.

April 19, 1934
Dear President:
Like Will Rogers I read the papers and read that you are having quite a lot of difficulty proving your fishing stories.

We had the same difficulty here for years and finally solved the problem by changing the standard measuring system to the Fisherman's rule. I'm enclosing one of these for your future fishing trips. Sorry that you had such difficulty during your present vacation.

This "Measuring Stick for Making the Little Fish Long Enough" (recommended and approved by Northwest Liars' Association for proving tall fish stories) reduced each inch by one-quarter.

A few months after his 1955 heart attack, Dwight Eisenhower received an Angler's Writ Of Absolution from a Hanover, Maine, couple. As members of the "Honorable Order of Expectant Bait Dunkers," they wrote in their cover letter,

> This is not a birthday and nor is it a "get well" card but just a note to let you know we think of you much and pray for your recovery.
>
> Whereas All Devotees of the Angler's Art are a Race apart; and Whereas Dwight David Eisenhower like all Fishermen, is prone to Over-estimate the Weight and Length of the One that got away, he has nevertheless, demonstrated his Proficiency with Rods, Reels, Flies, Spoons, Spinner, and other Piscatorial Impedimenta, thus Qualifying for Membership in the Honorable Order of Expectant Bait Dunkers and is a Member in Good Standing, is now and forever after shall be, ABSOLVED of Intentional Falsification and should he ever deign to relate a Fish Story that Smells like a Dead Mackerel after Long Exposure to the Sun, his Auditors will, by Virtue of his Possession of this Writ, accept his tale in Good Faith and graciously Attribute same to an Optical Illusion rather than to a vivid Imagination.

"Thirteen and a half inches," asserts presidential candidate Eisenhower to his running mate and the press as they relax in Fraser, Colorado, in July 1952. CORBIS-BETTMANN.

Dated in the City of Hanover Maine on this 11th Day of October, 1955.

In his sporting memoir, *An Outdoor Journal,* Jimmy Carter wrote that lying was doubtless practiced in the southern Georgia of his youth, but the moment of truth came when one had to display the catch.

"No one could get away with inflating his accomplishments; there were too many witnesses to the actual performance in this tiny community. For instance, a special string of trophy bass had to be displayed and weighed in the local grocery store in order to be believed."[14]

THE INFAMOUS "KILLER RABBIT"

Despite the admirable veracity he learned in Georgia, Jimmy Carter fell victim to a "fish story" that, if not concocted by the press, was at least abetted by the journalists. In the spring of 1979, Carter had gone back to

The Associated Press obtained a copy of this picture in June 1981 and wrote the following caption: "President Jimmy Carter makes a big splash as he fights off a 'killer rabbit' with an oar on a small pond near Plains, Georgia, April 21, 1979. The rabbit, which the President later guessed was fleeing in panic from some predator, actually swam toward his boat hissing menacingly, its teeth flashing and nostrils flared. Carter was not injured, and reports are unclear about what became of the Banzai Bunny." The photo was not released during Carter's presidency. AP/WIDE WORLD PHOTOS.

Plains for some rest. While he was fishing on a local pond, a swamp rabbit apparently swam out toward his boat. Carter shooed it off with a paddle.

The story remained a state secret until Brooks Jackson, an Associated Press writer, looking for something humorous to write during the dog days of August, stumbled onto it and got several staff members to confirm the story and even that a photo of the incident existed.

Jackson wrote the story, which made the front page of the *Washington Post* and dozens of other papers. Thus was born the tale of the "attack rabbit," and Carter's presidency would forever be associated with the Iranian hostage crisis, 20 percent inflation, and the Banzai Bunny.

According to political scientist Larry Sabato:[15]

> As Jackson recalled, I first heard the story in the spring of 1979 being floated around the White House and the staff was telling it about Carter. I confess I didn't see the significance.

The staff was pooh-poohing the story. Then Carter demanded that the White House photo shop make a blow-up of the picture. I never saw the picture, but in late August, I was assigned to write a humorous story, and I dug this thing out.

Well, the reaction astonished me, and I suspect it was because it was the perfect metaphor for that administration. The Carter White House [staff] embargoed the picture, so that it took the Reagan people to liberate the White House darkroom and release a print of the President and rabbit two years later.[16]

I will give the last word to Ed Zern, the late outdoor writer and humorist who wrote in *Field & Stream* in 1977,

There is, among hard-core fishermen, a conviction that truth, like pure water and the fish that live in it, is a precious commodity, not to be squandered or over-used. I respect that conviction and those who hold it. And if the philosophers ask, "What is truth?" I answer, "I haven't the foggiest notion, gents. But one thing it ain't is those stories you hear at Bud Lilly's or Phil Wright's or Dan Bailey's or any other tackle shop or fishing camp.

As for me, I get all the truth I need in the newspaper every morning, and every chance I get, I go fishing, or swap stories with fishermen, to get the taste of it out of my mouth.[17]

CHAPTER SEVEN

THE PEOPLE'S PEN PAL

July 20, 1936

Dear Mr. President,

I have seen from time to time that you take fishing trips every summer. I am a boy at the age of thirteen and have been working every [day] since June 5. I have made enough money to buy me a rod and reel and all the equipment to go with it. Is there any way that I could arrange to go with you. I could go anytime before September 1. Please write me wether I can go or not soon.

Jack Butler, Columbus, Ga.

White House aide Steve Early sent regrets, saying that although President Roosevelt would enjoy such an outing, the press of his duties prevented it.

Young Jack Butler had plenty of company in writing to the President about his fishing. Among the dozens of other people who wrote to FDR about his fishing just that summer was a man from Corbin, Kentucky, who asked FDR to contribute any spare fishing equipment to a private museum. (He could.) A New York advertising executive asked the President to contribute to a book of fishing experiences by "well-known Americans." (He couldn't.) That summer FDR received a $1.50 season fishing pass for the waters of Cisco Lake, Texas, and cast-by-cast accounts of the fishing experiences of a San Diego city councillor's children. Another man wrote to say he would be in Washington, D.C., soon and would "be happy to drop by the White House" to tell FDR about his fishing club.

One J. H. Sommers of Alabama City, Alabama, "a barber by trade, 54 years old, and a life-long Democrat, a Roosevelt Democrat," sent a studio portrait of himself and his catch of catfish, while a Sears and Roebuck store manager asked the President to write a short fishing story for a local contest. One correspondent offered to send FDR a tarpon he had just caught, while a company in India wanted to send the President free fishing equipment (FDR declined). Scores more letters were sent throughout his presidency. Some included snapshots of the proud angler-voters. Some politely invited the President on fishing trips; a few almost rudely demanded spare equipment. Franklin D. Roosevelt probably received more fishing-related letters than any other president, although the urge to communicate with the president has existed throughout the nation's history.

The American people have always been ambivalent about the role they want their presidents to play. They want the men to be both distant and approachable, to live in a mansion, yet talk over the back fence, to be equally comfortable on a yacht or a skiff. Fishing provides an opening for the average citizen to share something with that extraordinary institutional idol. Through common activities such as fishing, Americans can enter the White House on an equal footing. They can say to presidents who fish: "We have something in common; we know how you feel; we're buddies."

Such sentiments must have been on the mind of Archie R. Parker when he wrote Franklin D. Roosevelt on Jan. 4, 1937:

> Dear Sir,
>
> I am not writing you as President of the U.S.A. but as man to man and friend to friend.
>
> I love to fish and so do you. You are physically handicapped and so am I. That puts us in the same boat, so to speak, so lets pull a good oar together. I am writing you for a personal information. What length fishing pole do you like to fish with? What distance from butt of pole to real-seat [sic] do you like?
>
> Please send me this information and I will be happy and you will not be sorry.
>
> I like you an awful lot and all I ask is a chance to prove it, so don't disappoint me. (please).
>
> Wishing you a very happy and successful New Year I remain,
> Very respectfully yours,
> Archie R. Parker
> P.S. Enclosed find Air Mail Stamp for rapid transit.

Although Roosevelt relied on his staff to answer most of these letters, he made an exception in this case and dictated a note to his aide H. M. McIntyre: "Send him a line saying that I generally fish with the regulation salt-water rod, which has a long butt so that it can be put into either a belt or a socket in the seat. I do not know the length, but it is the regular salt-water-rod length."[1]

REQUESTS AND INVITATIONS

Through the decades hundreds of people have invited sitting presidents to go fishing, to donate used equipment, to visit their communities, to memorialize some local charity, and so on. Some letters have shown a familiarity usually reserved for close relations. The manager of the Hotel Marquette in Hot Springs, Arkansas, presumed on a past meeting to ask Roosevelt to write about his fishing for the benefit of a local radio audience.

My Dear Mr. President,

Having met you personally and chatted with you in your Warm Springs, Georgia, home in the year 1932, I feel at liberty to write you a personal letter, and I trust this letter will reach you, for it is nothing more than just a small personal matter.

Every Friday evening, at 6:50, I broadcast from KTHS station Hot Springs, on fishing, and what a fine recreation it is, and knowing you to be a lover of the sport of fishing, I would love to have a few words from you by letter, so that I may quote you in one of my broadcasts. . . .

Other letters were more deferential. A few days after the 1952 election, Mr. Grover Willcox of New London, Connecticut, wrote to ask Harry Truman to send two of his old fishing rods to give to two men too old to work. An aide wrote back to say that "much as he wishes it were possible to do this, the request is only one of many which come to the President every day. Unhappily, he cannot comply in each instance, and in order to be strictly impartial he has no alternative but to decline solicitations of this nature."

Invitations to fish were legion, and security concerns were always a good excuse for declining such offers. In July 1954, a persistent head of the Cotton Producers Association wrote to Eisenhower, promising to find him an accessible fishing spot near Augusta, Georgia, where the President liked to stay.

Eisenhower replied,

> Much as I should like to accept Dr. Pilcher's offer that I try
> out his lake, I am always confronted with the immense difficul-
> ties that are attendant whenever I visit a new location. There
> are so many problems involved that I frankly find it easier to
> stay within the confines of the Augusta National grounds. . . .

In 1988, private citizen Jimmy Carter joined several fly-fishing organi-
zations to fight government regulations governing a very specific
product. They argued that a U.S. Customs Service rule requiring each
imported fishing fly to carry an individual tag denoting the country of origin was manifestly cumbersome and destructive to the product. In a letter
to Treasury Secretary James Baker, himself a fly-fisherman, Carter wrote,
"Some of these flies are as small as a mosquito and this is an impractical
ruling. I hope you can help."[2]

Baker promised a careful review of the ruling, and observed in passing:

> As an avid (but too frequently inactive) sportsman, I read
> with particular interest your recent letter regarding country-of-
> origin marking requirements for imported fishing flies. Despite
> the great political debate over trade issues, I see no reason to let
> domestic fish have any advantage over domestic fishermen, if at
> all possible. . . .[3]

In less than a month, the Customs Service changed the ruling. The
bureaucratese is worth quoting,

> Section 304 of the Tariff Act of 1930, as amended (19 U.S.C.
> 1304) requires that, unless excepted, every article of foreign ori-
> gin imported into the United States shall be marked in a con-
> spicuous place as legibly, indelibly, and permanently as the
> nature of the article will permit in such a manner as to indicate
> to the ultimate purchaser the English name of the country of
> origin of the article. . . . Strict compliance with the marking
> statute would require that each individual fish fly be marked to
> indicate its country of origin. . . .
>
> Customs has now been presented with evidence establishing
> that those marking methods are impractical. Adhesive labels
> damage a fly by leaving residue on the feathers. String tags
> become hopelessly tangled while flies are grouped in retail bins

awaiting purchase. Placing flies in plastic bags is unacceptable since the tendency of the bag to return to its flat condition crushes the barbules of the feathers used on many patterns of flies. . . .

Other complications became evident. Even when a tag was affixed to a fly, its removal could damage the fly; the use of barbless hooks made the affixing of tags more difficult; an insurance company worried about the liability implications of selling flies in a condition where the hook had to be handled to remove a tag; removing the tag outdoors could contribute to the litter problem.

In addition to the difficulties caused by the various marking methods of labels, tags, and bagging outlines above, any of those methods interfere with two common tests performed by knowledgeable fly fisherman [sic] selecting flies from retail bins. First, the hackles or barbules are tested for desired firmness by gently stroking the fly with a fingertip or brushing the fly gently against the lips. Secondly, a properly tied and balanced fly should land upright when dropped onto a flat surface. Neither of these tests can be properly performed if flies are encumbered by labels or tags, or enclosed in plastic bags.

HOLDING:

Customs is now convinced that requiring individual marking of fishing flies is impractical. Therefore, pursuant to 19 U.S.C. 1304 (b) and Sec. 134.22, Customs Regulations, the outermost container or holder in which flies reach the ultimate purchaser shall be marked to indicate the country of origin of the flies. . . .[4]

In his cover letter to Carter, Baker announced the new ruling on country of origin and closed with the following: "Now that this impediment is removed, I hope you will be able to focus on the more challenging (and rewarding) task—getting the fish to bite!"

"This is a triumph of common sense over bureaucracy," Carter replied, "and a credit to you & the Customs officials! Thanks. Jimmy."[5]

OFFERS AND GIFTS

In their excitement about sharing a hobby with a president, some citizens went well beyond mere pen and paper. Some offered highly personal gifts, such as a certain reel willed to Grover Cleveland by his longtime fishing companion, the actor Joe Jefferson. When the gift was made public, James Buchan commemorated that gift in a poem in *Harper's Weekly*.

> Dear friend, I nevermore shall hear
> Your shout above the rushing stream,
> Nor see your struggling captive leap
> Where rainbows o'er the rapids gleam;
> But, ah! for sake of old lang syne,
> For sake of friendship long and leal,
> Take, with a comrade's lasting love,
> My best Kentucky reel.
>
> How oft your ardent eyes have said,
> "Ah me! how beautiful and rare,
> With music in its silken click,
> And graven with such loving care!"
> You never said, "I'd like it, Joe:
> I envy you from head to heel";
> But, Grover, well, I knew you craved
> My best Kentucky reel!
>
> And now it's yours, fond friend and best,
> Your undisputed own for aye;
> To sing to you beside the stream
> Through many a bloom-white April day—
> To sing, I fain, would think of me,
> When soft thoughts o'er your spirits steal
> And you can hear me prating of
> My best Kentucky reel.[6]

When *Century* magazine editor (and fishing crony of the President) Richard Gilder sent him a new reel, Cleveland replied,

Thanks for the new spinner. It strikes me as a killing device; and I am sure everything is fair against such a mean, tricky fish as the black bass. I am a little afraid that parts of the machine are too finely and delicately constructed to survive unimpaired a tough struggle with a vigorous bass; but I am going to a pond this afternoon where I know there are large fish and perhaps shall have the good fortune to test this matter.[7]

When reel maker Benjamin Milam sent a reel to Cleveland in 1887, the President wrote back that "I think it is the finest piece of work in that line I have ever seen and the sight and handling of it makes me long for the time when I can put it to use. . . ." Nine years later, during Cleveland's second term, the text of his letter showed up in a Milam Reels advertisement in *Forest & Stream* magazine, under the heading, "Read what President Cleveland thinks of the Frankfort Reel."[8]

Although he didn't fish nearly as much as Cleveland, Calvin Coolidge received numerous fishing-related gifts including books, flies, lures, and over twenty fly rods.

Jack Hallahan, a twelve-year-old boy from Landsdowne, Pennsylvania, sent Herbert Hoover some of his own flies and asked the President to trade. He told Hoover that his father had once received a fly from Coolidge. Hoover thanked the boy and sent him three flies in return.

At least one gift became an annual tradition. In 1912, an angler named Karl Anderson caught two salmon on opening day at the Bangor (Maine) salmon pool. One he sent to an industrialist in New Jersey. The second he sent to President William Howard Taft "to contribute to the city's need of honor and respect" for the President—Bangor having given its full complement of delegates to Taft at that year's Republican state convention. This was the beginning of the presidential salmon tradition, which saw the Penobscot Salmon Club buy the season's first salmon and send it to the White House for all but two years between 1912 and 1954.[9] (Interest in catching the first salmon depended in part upon the angler's (or bystander's) political persuasion. In 1938, Sylvia Ross, a die-hard Republican, was so upset at the thought of the salmon going to Franklin Roosevelt that she paid the premium price of $2.50 per pound for the first one caught, so that it would not be sent to Washington.)[10] The winner each year received a letter of congratulations from the president and had his or her name entered into the Salmon Club's record books. In 1916, the first salmon, a ten pounder, was caught by an angler who couldn't even vote— Miss Jeanette Sullivan of Bangor. Fifteen years earlier she had also caught the first salmon, one of sixteen and three-quarter pounds.[11]

In Hoover's first year in office, the Penobscot salmon duly arrived at the White House. A few days later, the directors of the fishing club themselves arrived, expecting to secure the chief executive's customary blessings and gratitude in a Rose Garden ceremony. Let Hoover tell the rest of the story:

Herbert Hoover puts on a brave face to receive the annual presidential salmon in 1931 from the man who caught it, Mr. Horace Chapman, president of the Bangor House hotel. From 1912 to 1952, the first salmon caught in the Bangor pool on the Penobscot River was sent to the sitting president. CORBIS-BETTMANN.

"Where is the salmon?" I asked a new and uninformed secretary. He replied that he had sent it to the White House kitchen and would get it back. He went to the kitchen to get the salmon but found that the cook had cut off its head and tail and otherwise prepared it for the oven. The intelligent cook was equal to the emergency. She sewed the head and tail on again and neatly stuffed it with cotton. The fish was brought out to the White House lawn. The secretary told me to hold it horizontally as it was very fragile. But one of the battery of photographers stepped up and said to me sotto voce that something was wrong with the fish. On hurried inspection, I found a large piece of cotton was sticking out of it.

A President must be equal to emergencies. I carefully held up the fish with my hand over the spot of cotton. The directors of the fishing club, the fish, and I posed before twenty photographers—and each posed for "just one more" six times. But the cotton kept oozing out of the fish as was proved by the later photographs. The fishing club did not use those later editions.[12]

On a fishing trip off Florida in March 1936, FDR caught a fish that could not immediately be identified. (It was later pegged as a species of amberjack.) The press made much of the mystery, and several citizens wrote with suggestions for identifying the species. An explosives manufacturer in Los Angeles offered a good deal more:

Dear Mr. President:

The morning papers and radio carried the news that you had caught a mysterious fish that was unknown and that you were returning it to the Smithsonian Institute in a block of ice.

Now, after twenty-two years of experimenting, we have developed an embalming fluid that will absolutely petrify a fish with all the natural color and shape.

Now, about your mysterious fish, I feel sure that you would like to have that embalmed perfectly, so that you could have it among your other trophies. We will gladly preserve same for you, free of charge, if you get the fish to us in a frozen condition and not spoiled. If you would be interested we will be glad to give your further data on the strange fish we are now preserving.

M. H. McEntyre, an assistant secretary to Roosevelt, replied:

[The President] greatly appreciates your kind offer to embalm the fish but as it has already been sent to the Smithsonian Institution for mounting, it will not be possible for him to avail himself of your kindness.

Mr. J. Frank Roberts Jr. of the R & R Live Bait Store in Columbus, Ohio, made an offer Roosevelt's aides also could refuse:

It has recently come to our attention that you are contemplating a fishing trip sometime this month.

With your kind permission, we would like to present to you, with our compliments, any bait you may need on your fishing trip.

If you wish, you may drop us a line telling us where you are going and what kind of fishing you expect to do, and we will have your bait sent directly to your destination.

For verification of the quality of our bait and our standing in this city, you may refer to either Congressman Lamneck or Senator Donahey, who are both old customers of ours.

[With best wishes,]

At the end of World War II John Heddon, president of the Heddon fishing tackle company—originators of the Heddon Liar's License—offered President Truman the initial fruit of peacetime conversion: the first fishing rod off the production line. Heddon would make it for whatever style the President preferred—salt water, fresh water, bait casting, fly fishing.

The task of declining fell to William Hassett, Truman's correspondence secretary:

May I say to you quite frankly that the President isn't much of a fisherman, and although he deeply appreciates your generous offer, the chances are that he will have very little time for the pursuit of Izaak Walton's art. As you know, the President is obliged to keep pretty close to his desk in Washington these days, and I am afraid there will be not very many opportunities for him to engage in fishing even if he were an enthusiast.

Sometimes the letters were hybrids—a gift combined with a request. In May 1950, a member of the Golden Bream Fishing Society of France wrote to President Truman. The State Department's translation follows:

In 1937 a group of local Waltonians established the "Golden Bream Fishing Society." They worked hard to get their fishing stream well stocked and had just got it in good condition when the war broke out, and during the war years the stream was ruined. Now they are again working to fix up the stream, but unfortunately, while before the war they could do many fine things with the franc, it now takes many francs to do small

things. The Society sends the President an honorary membership card entitling him to fish in the stream in 1950 and offer
him the honorary vice presidency. The members will be happy
to receive any contribution he may care to make to the re-
establishment of the stream for good fishing.

Again, Truman's aides declined.

President Eisenhower's evident love of fishing spawned hundreds of
gifts of flies, equipment, lures, rods, and, in some cases, even fish. By the
third year of his first term, Eisenhower had accumulated between eight
hundred and one thousand individual gifts of rods, reels, flies, spinners, and
the like. The donors were of all ages.

Some of the flies had unique names such as "Sputnik chaser," "61-
Chevy car-styling," "Uncle Sam fly," and "God's River Streamers." He
received several recipes for "Trout Eisenhower." The famous hotelier
Charles Ritz sent him two fly rods. People sent salmon-egg dispensers,
synthetic fish eggs, a "Fish-catcher" with bell and spring to alert the fisherman, "Detty's Fish-Gripper," "Lucky Strike Minnows," "Langley's Fisherman De-Liar," and numerous others. In most cases, the staff replied, but
Eisenhower sent a personal note to a correspondent from Provo, Utah:

I am intrigued by the fishing flies you sent me the other day. I must
admit that the use of Miss Eccles' red hair in making these flies is a rather
unusual idea. Thank you for sending them, and for expressing good wishes
in my using them.

A 1955 magazine cover story on Eisenhower's fishing spurred several
people to write about the President's technique. One man in Arkansas
chided Eisenhower for having so much slack line. "As our nations Executive Leader you are unexcelled. But—as a Fly Fisherman, just how do you
SET the hook when a fish strikes. . . . Maybe you use an automatice [sic]
reel or depend on the Atom, to take up all that slack line, with your left
hand in that position. Mr. President, fish strike fast."

Governor Milward Simpson of Wyoming had another purpose in
mind when he wrote:

Recently I read in Colliers Magazine the very interesting article about
you and your fly fishing. Having been an ardent devotee of this sport all
my life, I was naturally quite interested.

While attending a Pardon Board meeting at our State Penitentiary at Rawlins, Wyoming, a nice looking boy appeared for commutation of his sentence. In questioning him I discovered that he professed to be a very capable tyer of flies. I bought the Colliers Magazine and asked him to duplicate the flies on the cover and to furnish me with some of his own making. To my amazement he sent me some flies that are of excellent construction and exhibit beautiful handiwork.

I immediately thought of you and your hobby. With your approval, I am asking the young man to tie a similar number of these beautiful flies, which are going to be sent to you within the next week or so. I want you to be on the alert for the package because I think you are going to be mighty pleased and surprised when you see this demonstration of expertness on the part of this young fellow. I want you to have these flies with my compliments.

With expressions of personal regard and esteem.

Eisenhower replied two weeks later:

Dear Governor Simpson:

The flies tied by one of the inmates of your State Penitentiary arrived in my office this morning, and I quite agree with you that they are beautifully made. If the art of fly tying is a part of the rehabilitation program offered at Rawlins, certainly you and the prison officials are to be congratulated.

Quite naturally, my curiosity is aroused. Did the young man get the pardon?

My thanks are due to you and to the artist who made the flies. I am hoping to get a little fishing trip in one of these days and I shall take this box along with me.

The prisoner, convicted of manslaughter, did have his sentence commuted from ten to fifteen years to one and a half to five years. He was paroled on April 20, 1955.[13]

To help President Eisenhower recover from his 1955 heart attack, the celebrated fly tyer and writer Joe Bates sent him a copy of his book *Trout Waters and How to Fish Them*. Eisenhower replied: "Your thoughtfulness makes me all the more impatient once again to fish one of my favorite streams; at the same time, the book will give me the opportunity of experiencing, by remote control, the delights of the sport we both enjoy so much."[14]

While on a fishing trip to Yellowstone National Park, Jimmy Carter met Don Daughenbaugh, a high school teacher from Williamsport, Pennsylvania, who spent his summers as a fly-fishing specialist in the Yellowstone area. Daughenbaugh had given Rosalynn Carter one of her first fly-fishing lessons on the Snake River in Idaho, and he had become a fast friend of the First Family. In no time he and the President were corresponding about the important things in life, such as fly line and fly patterns. From Moran, Wyoming, he wrote to the President in June 1980:

Dear Mr. Carter,

Let me first congratulate you on your entry into the fly tying fraternity. You are now hooked, and your life will never be the same. In fact, the fish will probably be wiped out around Camp David now that they will be seeing flies with a Southern flair.

I am enclosing a fly-tying book that you can share with your son, Jack, if you so desire. I start my fly tying classes at the College with this text because it is so well illustrated. The following book is more advanced and a favorite of mine.

Popular Fly Patterns
by Terry Hellekson
Peregrine Smith, Inc.
Salt Lake City, 1977

The above is a great book for patterns in the East and West and shows lots of new techniques as well as materials used. You will find that fly tying is nothing more than learning tricks and methods that change from tyer to tyer. Materials change from text to text, but I find that natural furs seem to make the more productive fly. I have lots at home, and if you are not too much in a hurry, I will see that you get lots of fox, elk, and other furs that are superior.

I suppose you are looking forward to wetting a line in California. It may be wise to get a double-tapered wet #6 line for your Leonard rod in case there is a little dry-fly action. I have learned many years ago in fishing Western waters that in order to consistently catch trout you must fish wet flies and nymphs. Larger rods also can be used to a great advantage. Otherwise, you spend a lot of time looking for rising fish or searching for streams where good hatches are in progress. Once the fish become surface minded, it usually continues for the rest of the season.

I generally start with a rig of three flies when fishing wet and always tie my own leaders. Just tie your blood knot with extra long ends. Cut off the one side, and attach your fly to the dropper.

Sometimes I fish only one fly, especially on nymphs. Hope you have a great trip West and have many tight lines.

Carter sent a hand-written reply on July 2, 1980:

To Don Daughenbaugh

Thank you, again!

My sons & I had a great 24 hours at Spruce Creek (we fished 16 of them), & since then I've been trying to match some of the beauty of your flies. Last Sat. Rosalynn & I went to a small stream above Thurmont where the caretaker said they wouldn't take a dry—only a few on a Tellico (?) [sic] nymph. I caught about 20 browns on an Irresistible & Rosalynn kept an 18" rainbow [that] swallowed her fly. I can't go to California, but will try one day with Gov. Hammond in Alaska & will find a North Ga. stream for trout & some S. Ga ponds for bream & bass.

Your friend, Jimmy (fly tyer)

In 1984, Vice President Bush went to Vermont as the keynote speaker for a dinner to reelect Ronald Reagan. A few days before the speech, Farrow Allen, who owned a fly-fishing shop in South Burlington, got a call from the state Republican committee to say that the Orvis Company had donated a fly rod to be presented to Bush, and they would like to get a reel to go with it. Allen continues the story:

> That was fine, I told them. A few days later in came a man and a woman with the rod, looking for the reel. I recognized her as a state senator from southern Vermont. The rod was a light saltwater style for bluefish. I pulled out a Hardy Marquis reel that I thought would fit well.
>
> "How much?" she asked. When I told her it was $125.00, she snorted, "That's too much. Haven't you got anything cheaper?"
>
> I reached down on a shelf and pulled out a Scientific Anglers reel for $80. That was still too expensive, she said. So I went to the bottom shelf and brought out a Martin MG-7. It was $39.95.

"I'll take it!" she said quickly.

I asked her what kind of line should I put on the reel.

She looked at me as if I had insulted her. "I think the vice president can afford to buy his own line!"

"OK. Shall I wrap it?" I asked.

"No, the Secret Service will have to look inside anyway!"

And that was it. She ordered the man [with her] to pay for the reel—cash—and they rushed out of the store as they had raced in. And ever after that Martin MG-7 was known as the vice presidential reel.[15]

THIS IS THE WHITE HOUSE CALLING

Dean Minton is a commercial artist and caricaturist in Panama City Beach, Florida. To draw sidewalk business, he displays drawings of former customers as well as cartoons of famous people. In 1989, when President George Bush went fishing off the Florida Keys, Minton drew a cartoon of him. After it hung in his shop for several weeks, Minton's wife Mary suggested that he send it to the White House. Minton was skeptical that anyone would even acknowledge the gift, but he sent it anyway. He tells what happened next.

"Why is this taking so long?" whined the boy sitting opposite my drafting table.

The phone rang just as I finished the ink sketch of the squirming seven-year-old who dreamed of playing major league baseball.

"Cartoons by Deano," I said into the phone.

A female voice replied: "This is the White House calling."

I pinched the phone between my ears and shoulder while mixing watercolor on my paint palette. "Who?"

"The White House. We received your caricature of President Bush, and we really like it."

"Oh, uh, good." Two weeks before my wife had impulsively sent the White House a cartoon of the President that we had displayed in our shop. I never expected any response or acknowledgment. "Since I work in a popular tourist spot in Florida, I thought I'd draw our latest distinguished visitor when he came down for some bonefishing after winning the election.

He's about to get tied up with problems of the deficit and the savings and loan thing, and"—flesh tones dripped from my suspended brush as I rattled on—and, uh, there's President Reagan floating away and giving him advice—"

"It's a good likeness," broke in the female voice. "What's the cartoon's value?"

"Oh, priceless," I said, still not sure the call was legit. I concentrated on applying paint to the fidgeting ball player's picture.

"Of course, but can you give us a dollar amount?"

"Oh, how 'bout thirty?"

"Thirty what?" she persisted.

"Million," I said playfully.

Silence. I dipped my brush and applied more paint. More silence.

My thoughts raced through the void. The giddiness of getting a phone call from the White House faded. She knew I was kidding, didn't she? She didn't think I was trying to buy presidential influence, did she? Dark visions grew of FBI agents interrogating me in a cellar room.

"Just what did you expect to accomplish with this gift, Mr. Minton? Does your company now or has it ever had any contracts with the government, Mr. Minton? Have you ever protested any government policy, Mr. Minton? . . ."

I started to sweat.

"What, again, was the value of your gift?" asked the woman with just a trace of annoyance.

"Thirty dollars," I blurted out.

"Excuse me?" she asked.

I cleared my throat and mixed a new color as the seven-year-old strained to see his likeness.

"Just thirty dollars," I repeated.

"Well, thank you, Mr. Minton. We're adding your cartoon to the presidential library."

After hanging up the phone, I beamed and told the boy with conspiratorial pride, "You know, that was the White House calling."

"Why is this taking so long?" was all he said.[16]

CARPING, PRAISE, AND ADVICE

As we have seen with Coolidge and the worm controversy, president-anglers were not immune to criticism for their techniques. The right to vote has always granted the right to criticize. Presidents have been excoriated for everything from boorishness to corruption. Grumbling in 1882 that presidents took overly long vacations, Charles Dana, editor of the *New York Sun,* sent one of his top reporters to document such idleness. If Chester A. Arthur was determined to fish instead of work, the *Sun* declared, then Congress should pass a law that cut a president's pay when he was on vacation.[17]

When Grover Cleveland endured similar criticisms, he was unrepentant.

> [These] petty forms of persecution [are] . . . nothing more serious than gnat stings suffered on the bank of a stream. . . . When short fishing excursions, in which I have sought relief from the wearing labors and perplexities of official duty, have been denounced in a mendacious newspaper as dishonest devices . . . I have been able to enjoy a sort of pleasurable contempt for the author of this accusation, while congratulating myself on the mental and physical restoration I had derived from these excursions. . . . [S]o far as my attachment to outdoor sports may be considered a fault, I am . . . utterly incorrigible and shameless.[18]

Harder to dismiss was the criticism of the clergy. A minister from Upper Darby, Pennsylvania, wrote to rebuke President Hoover for not keeping the Sabbath holy:

Dear Sir,

We prayed for you in our church last Lord's day, that a conviction might come to your mind that you are not giving the nation the proper example of observing the Lord's day by going fishing on the one day of the week that God has asked us to give to him. What would be the condition in this great nation if everyone did as you are doing on the Lord's day?

Hoover's aide Lawrence Richey tried to mollify the perturbed parson:

My dear Doctor [*sic*], Your letter of May 20th has been received. The President's week-end trips to the mountains are for the purpose of securing rest and relaxation. He never fishes on Sunday.

Commercial artist Dean Minton sent the enclosed "Deano" cartoon of George Bush to the White House in celebration of Bush's periodic Florida fishing. GEORGE BUSH PRESIDENTIAL LIBRARY.

Near the end of Hoover's term, Dr. Edward T. Curran of New York City wrote to tell the President that he didn't fish enough:

You ought to do something to stop the publicity of those fishing trips of yours.

Those of us, these days chained to the desk, dream of days to come when no jealousy will occur towards the catches they say you are getting.

Nothing to beat it for relaxation and pleasure—and you need it. Good luck.

However gloating over every detail of size, number, and I might almost say the smell and taste of the savory fish: well; I think it's rather mean—don't you?

Hoover's reply showed that the criticism had affected him.

My dear Dr. Curran,

After two modest attempts in seventeen months to catch fish, I find that public duties will prevent me from any further efforts in that direction. I would like to call your attention to the fact that prayer and fishing are the only two purely personal relations [sic] of the President of the United States the privacy of which is respected by the public at large. An occasional fishing expedition, with its communion with the sea and the streams, thus has refreshing possibilities for public duty.

Nevertheless, despite all of this, I am convinced that during the next few months there will be no opportunity for any further gloating as the result of my feats, sad as that may be.[19]

Franklin D. Roosevelt took his share of criticism for fishing too much and catching too little. Harry P. Taylor, president of the Taylor Bros. Tobacco Co. of Winston-Salem, North Carolina, came to his defense:

Honorable Franklin D. Roosevelt, Fisherman,
The White House
Washington, D.C.
Most Honorable Sir:—In Re: Fishing

May I avail myself of the privilege of coming to your defense, sir?

I justly resent the implied and unwarranted aspersions cast upon you as a fisherman.

It is not "the fish you catch" but the spirit in which you catch your fish that really counts.

There are those who may catch fish and yet be devoid of the true spirit of fisherman. There are those who may catch fish and yet fail to be true exponents of the real art of fishing. There is a subtle yet distinct and well defined difference between those who lack genuine sportsmanship and those who are the honored and blessed possessors of that priceless gift of honest and genuine sportsmanship.

Allow me to congratulate you, sir, and humbly render honor to whom honor is due. Carping critics of a true fisherman are but those who, in their ignorance, talk the most about that of which they know the least. May the Good God pity them in their soul-starved ignorance. To contemplate, to relax in retrospect. To experience that peace of mind, that comfort and joy of heart and soul and being—a cleaning and freeing of the cobwebs of care from a weary mind, a purification of the soul—the essence of true and genuine happiness.

This, then, is the gift of the Gods to all true fishermen. Again, sir, let me congratulate you upon the possession of this well deserved gift. Nurture it, preserve it, free from contamination, that it may grow and fill your being and you, thus, grow in grace.

Sincerely,

A humble, yet reverent, member of the Ranks of Those Who Fish.

s/Harry P. Taylor

Roosevelt received advice on both obtaining and using bait. One man from New York City, hearing that FDR was fishing off the west coast of Panama, wrote to suggest "[t]wo charges of T.N.T., using slow fuse, when exploded on an incoming tide will provide plenty of bait." Another man advised FDR on how to stimulate bluefish by using "sardines very much smashed up in the oil and spread over the course. . . . I suggest you take along a few tins of the cheapest Portuguese variety obtainable."

In June 1955, Representative Henry Reuss (D—Wisconsin) sent Ike a column from the educational director of the Dane County Humane Society, Mr. Alexius Baas. The column was an open letter to the President:

> You need hardly be told that by virtue of your great office you are constantly in the public eye and that every thing you do, in or out of your official capacity, is scrutinized by many millions of people old and young. Your influence, whether you

exert it consciously or unconsciously, is tremendous. Millions of boys in this and other countries regard you with such hero worship as to put into your hands the power to mold them for good or evil. The victorious general, great soldier, and President of our country can, in their eyes, do no wrong.

All of this is but a prologue to the principal theme of this little essay which for want of a better or more fitting title might be called "Kindness to Animals."

In common with millions of other Americans, I have noted that you spend your vacations in the open, gun or fishing rod in hand, killing as many of the little creatures of field, forest, and stream as the law will permit. No one questions your right—even your duty—to get away from the crushing obligations of your office as often as possible. Neither does anyone question your right to assume the questionable role of sportsman. You have the right under the law to kill and wound inoffensive wild life to the limit of your powers as a marksman—under human law, that is. . . .

Baas went on to ask rhetorically if there isn't a "higher law" that calls for mercy.

Your profession, Mr. President, before you became president, was that of a soldier. Like all great soldiers you hate the cruelty attendant upon war. Can you not extend that hatred of cruelty to take in animal life, as well? Think what an influence for kindness and mercy you could bring to bear upon the children of this country, yes of all countries, by throwing rod and gun away and substituting gentleness and love for slaughter and torture. . . .[20]

Another salvo of fishing criticism of Eisenhower came in the form of a telegram:

The Rhode Island League of Salt Water Anglers, an organization dedicated to the preservation of the salt water resources of the nation, is appealing to you as the number one sportsman of the nation to intervene in the wholesale chumming of the Newport waters in a desperate effort to entice stripped [sic] bass and other game species into those waters for your fishing pleasure. . . .[21]

Ike's press secretary, James C. Hagerty, replied to the league:

> As you undoubtedly have read by now, I have already made a
> statement that the chumming of the Newport waters was done
> entirely without the President's knowledge—and all of us here
> at the White House don't like it anymore than you do.[22]

After the election of 1980, the author William Humphrey sent a copy
of his short book on salmon fishing *(The Spawning Run)* to Jimmy Carter
in the White House with the following note:

Dear Mr. President, I'm sorry you lost the election. I did my part to
keep you in office. I don't know why anyone would want that job.

I saw in the paper that your ambition now is to become a good fly-
fisherman. You'll find that harder than governing the country—it's
upstream all the way. Sincerely,[23]

Shortly before his death in 1964, Herbert Hoover received an enquiry
about his fishing habits from a young girl.

Dear Mr. Hoover,
    I am ten years old.
    The papers say you go fishing. I do to [sic]. What
    kind of fish do you get? I prefer catfish. What
    bait do you use? I use worms.
Love, Mary

Hoover replied:

My dear Mary,
    I have fished whenever I had a chance for over eighty-seven years. I
hope you will also. It is good for you. When I was your age I lived in a
trout region. I also fished with worms, but a kindly man gave me three
artificial flies. I used them successfully until all the wing feathers were worn
off. Nowadays I mostly fish for bonefish with a live shrimp for bait. Bonefish are not good to eat. I put them back in the water so they can grow
bigger. Bonefishing around the Florida Keys is especially adapted to elderly
gentlemen who can no longer clamber among the rocks and the brush.
Keep this in mind when you are eighty-seven.[24]

CHAPTER EIGHT

PRESIDENTS, FISHING, AND SWEARING

Guess I'm a real fisherman now. I cussed!   —*Calvin Coolidge*

A fisherman must be of contemplative mind," wrote Herbert Hoover, "for it is often a long time between bites. Those interregnums emanate patience, reserve, and calm reflection—for no one can catch fish in anger, or in malice. He is by nature an optimist or he would not go fishing. . . ."[1]

It was easy for him to say, in the tolerant twilight of his life. But show me the angler who has never lost a fish, and I'll show you an angler who has never caught one. Show me an angler who has never sworn, and I'll show you one who is devoid of emotion—and one who has probably caught few fish. Swearing is to fishing as flowers are to spring, and when it comes to fishing and swearing, presidents are mere mortals. And a good thing it is that they and we can let go. As the inimitable political commentator Finley Peter Dunne (Mr. Dooley) remarked in a broader context, "[T]h' best thing about a little judicyous swearin' is that it keeps th' temper. Twas intinded as a compromise between runnin' away an' fightin'. Before it was invinted they was the on'y two ways out iv an argymint."[2]

Before he was president, Chester A. Arthur did much fishing for Atlantic salmon and even held a record of fifty-one pounds on the Cascapedia River in Quebec. On one occasion when fishing with the writer George Dawson, he lost a fish to the ineptitude of the guide.

Arthur had hooked the fish and brought it into shallow water, where it lay seemingly dead. The guide struck at it with the gaff once, twice, thrice with no effect, except that he broke the leader. Even then the fish didn't move. The guide tried once more.

> But before the gaff fell where the fish was, he wasn't there,
> and thirty-five pounds of as fine salmon as ever wagged a tail

THE GENERAL FIGHTING A THIRTY-FOUR POUND FISH.

George Dawson, our first fly-fishing columnist and author of probably the first book in America dedicated to fly-fishing, counted among his friends two presidents and a vice president. In a woodcut from his book, The Pleasures of Angling, *the future president is about to lose a salmon to the guide's ineptitude.*

floated off with the current, in all probability to die "unwept, unhonored, and unsung." Expletives, like notes of music, are modulated to meet the intensity of the emotions. The General's expletive was pitched on the upper register, and the gaffer would have been pitched into the Cascapedia if he hadn't looked as if that was just what he expected.[3]

Calvin Coolidge was modest enough about his fishing to see that his enthusiasm exceeded his ability. According to Edmund Starling, Coolidge's Secret Service chief and fishing mentor, the President was fishing one day on the Brule River in Wisconsin. He lost "a fish he had been playing, and I heard him say, 'Damn!' Then he turned to me and with a shy smile said: 'Guess I'm a real fisherman now. I cussed.' "[4]

Franklin D. Roosevelt loved to fish. Because of his handicap, he was never able to fish alone. He tried to show the public that these fishing expeditions were all easy plain fun and good times, and any competition was of the most innocent sort. In the introduction to his Jefferson Day speech in 1941, he observed, "That means that if today the fellow next to

The cartoonist H. T. Webster poses a delicious dilemma for the legendarily taciturn Calvin Coolidge when a fish breaks his line. NEW YORK HERALD TRIBUNE, 1926. ALL RIGHTS RESERVED.

you catches a bigger fish than you do, and vice versa, you don't lie awake at night thinking about it. . . ."[5]

Yet according to John Gunther, some of these competitions could get out of hand. "Leon Henderson [whom Roosevelt had appointed head of the Office of Price Administration] is, so far as I know, the only man alive who ever called the President a blank-of-a-blank to his face and got away with it. The occasion was a dispute during a fishing trip over the size of the catch. . . ."[6]

When Aksel Nielsen, an Eisenhower fishing crony, was asked if Ike ever lost a fish, he replied, "You betcha he does. Just like anybody else."

What then? "Well, let's put it this way. If Ike loses a fish, he has more than a few well-chosen words at his command to express his disappointment. After all, he was in the army for forty-odd years."[7]

Fishing once with friends in Pennsylvania, Jimmy Carter recorded what he called his "most frustrating fishing experience." The weather was perfect that evening, but everything else went wrong—equipment broke, tippets snapped, he forgot his flashlight so he couldn't tie on smaller flies, trees and bushes snagged his casts, and he caught nothing.

Engineer that he was, he spent the next morning assessing all his mistakes, disassembling all his equipment, laying in a new store of leaders, and tying a new batch of flies. As the next day was Sunday, "everyone was convinced that I needed to go to church."

That night he returned to the same spot and minutes later, hooked a large trout. He fought it for a few minutes, then proudly called out to Rosalynn. The trout chose that moment to take off downstream and hide in an underwater pile of trash. Carter worked the trout out slowly and was just about to net it when the fish broke the leader. "For a few moments I forgot the church sermon and my Baptist training and said some choice words that disturbed the former quiet of the murmuring stream."[8]

Grover Cleveland had the masterly talent for turning the baser instincts into the higher purpose. Let him have the last words.

[The opponents of fishing] have not been content, however, in demonstration of their evil-mindedness without adding to their indictment against the brotherhood the charge of profanity. Of course, they have not the hardihood to allege that our profanity is of that habitual and low sort [that] characterizes the coarse and ill-bred, who offend all decent people by constantly interlarding their speech with fearful and irrelevant oaths. They,

WITHOUT BENEFIT OF TELE-PROMPTER.

There was nothing like a snarled line or a lost fish to spur Dwight Eisenhower to speak his mind to fish and the heavens, according to cartoonist Ed Kuekes. CLEVELAND
PLAIN-DEALER.

nevertheless, find sufficient excuse for their accusations in the sudden ejaculations, outwardly resembling profanity, [that] are occasionally wrung from fishermen in trying crises and in moments of soul-straining unkindness of Fate.

Now, this question of profanity is largely one of intention and deliberation. The man who, intending what he says, coolly indulges in imprecation, is guilty of an offense that admits of no excuse or attenuation; but a fisherman can hardly be called profane who, when overtaken without warning by disaster, and abruptly hurled from the exhilarating heights of delightful anticipation to the depths of dire disappointment, impulsively gives vent to his pent-up emotion by the use of a word [that], though found in the list of oaths, is spoken without intentional imprecation and because nothing else seems to suit the occasion. It is by no means to be admitted that fishing tends even to this semblance of profanity. On the contrary, it imposes a self-restraint and patient forbearance upon its advanced devotees, which tends to prevent sudden outbursts of feeling.

It must in frankness be admitted, however, by fishermen of every degree, that when the largest trout of the day, after a long struggle, winds the leader about a snag and escapes, or when a large salmon or bass, apparently fatigued to the point of non-resistance, suddenly, by an unexpected and vicious leap, frees himself from the hook, the fisherman's code of morals will not condemn beyond forgiveness the holder of the straightened rod if he impulsively, but with all the gentility at his command, exclaims: "Damn that fish!" It is probably better not to speak at all; but if strong words are to be used, perhaps these will serve as well as any that can do justice to the occasion.[9]

CHAPTER NINE

THE FISHING CABINETS

No man can be a completely good fisherman unless within his piscatorial sphere he is generous, sympathetic, and honest . . . generous to the point of willingness to share his last leaders and flies, or any other items of his outfit, with any worthy fellow-fisherman who may be in need.[1]　　—Grover Cleveland

Fishermen are gregarious. Otherwise, the mighty deeds of the day or of a year ago or of ten years ago would go unsung. No one but fishermen will listen to them. Therefore, as two or three are gathered together, the spiritual vitamins of faith, hope, and charity have constant regeneration.[2]　　—Herbert Hoover

Sitting in a small bateau in our own farm pond, choosing for our supper the mature bluegills and bass we've caught and returning the others to grow some more, gives us long and precious hours of uninterrupted conversation about all kinds of things, an opportunity quite rare in the lives of many married couples.[3]　　—Jimmy Carter

Longtime White House usher Irwin Hoover once observed that most presidents had their recreational cabinets. While Teddy Roosevelt had a tennis cabinet, Woodrow Wilson a golf cabinet, and Warren Harding a poker cabinet, Grover Cleveland had his fishing cabinet, which consisted of the financier E. C. Benedict and his private secretary, Henry T. Thurber, the editor Richard Gilder, and the actor Joe Jefferson.[4] In the third year of his disastrous second term, beset by strikes, clashes with his own party, international disputes in Hawaii and Venezuela, Cleveland was still able to pen a tongue-in-cheek letter to Jefferson about some fine fishing near Buzzards Bay, Massachusetts.

I am told that you sometimes find recreation in the rod and
reel. I think it not amiss, therefore, to suggest a locality or spot
where you might be able to find some sport in the direction

mentioned. On the Sandwich road, a mile or two from Bourne, is a sort of abandoned farm, now owned by that universally popular veteran comedian Joseph Jefferson. This farm was originally purchased, I think, by Mr. Jefferson on account of a trout stream running through it; but lately he seems to have lost conceit with it and now pretty much neglects it. I am told he is a little capricious that way.

However, we will let that pass, since a friend visiting me and I took eight (8) as handsome trout as you would wish to see in a whole season out of that selfsame stream, this afternoon, in a short time. At the point where a railroad crosses the stream seems to be the spot where the fish congregate—though other places near-by will yield good results. Almost anybody about Bourne can tell you where the Jefferson farm is; and I am sure the owner would not object to your fishing there.[5]

And in a further letter, he observed that what mattered on these trips was not the catch but the company. "Did it ever occur to you what a fortunate thing it is that you and I jointly are able to appreciate and enjoy a regular out-and-out outing, undisturbed by the question of fish captured? How many of our excursions have been thus redeemed!"[6]

This chapter deals with what might be called the social side of presidential fishing. On these expeditions, the presidents and fishing cronies shared moments of high hope and low disappointment. They told and retold their ancient tales of success and failure. They engaged in lively and loud competitions and quietly swapped advice and equipment. They traded insults and praise. Together, they marveled at nature. These fishing cronies stoutly defended the presidents from the arrows of press, public, and other politicians. No president was betrayed at fishing camp.

These presidential fishing buddies were (and are) a diverse lot. Some were close advisers who fished incidentally, such as FDR's aides Harry Hopkins and Basil O'Connor or Carter's press secretary, Jody Powell, or Bush's National Security Adviser, Brent Scowcroft. Others were utterly nonpolitical such as Cleveland's buddy Joe Jefferson, the actor, and Ken Raynor, a Maine golf pro who fishes with George Bush. Some were family, such as Ike's brothers, Rosalynn Carter, George Bush's sons and grandsons. And others were guides who, with emotions ranging from awe and friendship to self-importance and disdain, showed the presidents how and where to fish.

THEODORE ROOSEVELT, RUSSELL COLES, AND
DEVILFISH
In his 1920 book, *Talks with T.R.*, John J. O'Leary transcribed an interview
with Roosevelt on devilfishing.

"Good sport, but not exactly the thing to recommend to a
weakling, or one at all nervous of a little danger," was Colonel
Teddy Roosevelt's opinion of devilfishing. He had one try at
this, in the spring of 1917 [off the coast of Florida], when the
declaration of war against Germany made it seem advisable to
call off a visit to the West Indies for which he had made all his
plans.

He thought so well of the sport that just before he died he
wrote his friend Russell J. Coles, of Danville, Virginia, accept-
ing an invitation to join him in an expedition on March 1, and
thanking him for having included Captain Archie, then practi-
cally recovered from his wounds, in the invitation.

"The devil fish," said the Colonel describing the sport in his
library at Oyster Bay, "is the big game of the sea. There is nothing else quite like it that I know of, though I doubt if it will
ever become a very popular sport. It is good sport, but not
exactly the kind to recommend to a weakling, or one at all nervous of a little danger. I do not know that careful physicians will
agree in recommending it to gentlemen of advanced years, for,
as you may imagine, it is hard work.

"I became interested in devil-fishing through Russell Coles,
of Danville, Virginia. Coles is rather an extraordinary sort of
person, the unusual combination of good business man and
high-class scientist. Most of his year he devotes to his tobacco
business in Virginia. The rest of it he puts in hunting devil fish
and sharks, and by way of diversion at odd moments writes scientific articles, or prepares papers to be read at scientific soci-
eties. He takes a very practical interest in public affairs, and is in
every sense of the word a mighty fine citizen.

"I became interested in him through something he did for
the American Museum of Natural History. That was some years
ago. Since then I have had much correspondence with him, and
when I found that I could not go South as I had arranged, I
decided to accept one of his many invitations to go fishing. His

proposal was that I should spend a month. We compromised on about a week.

"In devil-fishing you camp in a house built on a scow that is anchored off a Florida key. Your fishing you do from a launch. Coles, who is a whale of a man himself, has a crew that is as good as he is. His captain, Charley Willis, is a powerful, two-handed sort of a man who has been with him many years. Another of his outfit is Captain Jack McCann. He's unusual, too, a good seaman and a naturalist, who habitually describes plants by their scientific names. The others of his crew—he usually has four men—are of the same high type of intelligence.[*]

"It is some considerable journey to the camp. There you get up at sunrise, get into rough clothes, and after you have made sure the gear is all right, make off in the launch for the fishing grounds. The weapons used are harpoons, which the real fishermen call 'irons,' just as I have heard some whalers call their weapons, and a lance. Sometimes the old-fashioned whaling lance is used. Coles has had some made on designs of his own. New Bedford, by the way, is the best place to get these things if you ever wish for them.

"The iron is a business-like weapon. It has a head of the finest tempered steel, on a shaft of soft iron. There is one there, minus the wooden handle. When you see the way that is bent, you will see why it is necessary to make the shaft of comparatively soft metal."[7]

The instrument, somewhat rusted, was bent to an angle of almost forty-five degrees and occupied a place of honor on the mantel on which rested the bronze presented to him by the famous "tennis cabinet."

---

[*]In an article in *Scribner's* magazine, Roosevelt, long a critic of Woodrow Wilson's pacifism, described the crew in patriotic terms:
"These four men, who composed the actual crew, were Americans of a kind that we like to regard as typical—the type welcome to the soul that has become heartsick over the moral degeneracy implied in the decadent sentimentality of professional pacifism and the revolting and sordid grossness of its ally materialism. All four were professional fishermen, averaging fifty years of age. They were alert, weather-beaten men who all their lives long had wrought their livelihood by hard and hazardous labor on the sea. They were quiet, hard-working, self-reliant, utterly fearless. . . ."[8]

Theodore Roosevelt with Russell Coles on their 1917 outing to hunt devilfish.
THEODORE ROOSEVELT COLLECTION, HARVARD COLLEGE LIBRARY.

The next year Roosevelt and Coles both received honorary degrees from Trinity College in Connecticut. THEODORE ROOSEVELT COLLECTION, HARVARD COLLEGE LIBRARY.

Theodore Roosevelt and Russell Coles with harpoons and devilfish.
THEODORE ROOSEVELT COLLECTION, HARVARD COLLEGE LIBRARY.

"That's one I used on the big fish I got with Coles' assistance. You see it is so built that once in, the struggles of the beast release the barb and usually, though not always, prevents your prey [from] escaping. The iron is attached to a rope, which is either run out of the boat or made fast to what they call a drogue—a sort of sea anchor, or drag. This is a powerful brake, but one of these creatures will pull a heavy launch almost unbelievable distances with one of these drogues fastened to it with another harpoon.

"I missed my first fish through inexperience in gauging the speed at which it was moving. The second one, I got square in the middle of the body. When we came to take my iron out, we found I had driven it through bone, muscle, and hide more than two feet—two feet four inches to be exact—and the thing had gone through the beast's heart. After I got my iron into it, Coles also put one in. With these two in its body, the thing dragged the boat a full half-mile before it became exhausted enough for us to get it alongside. Then it was necessary to use the lance on it twice.

"I should say that before I went to Florida, Coles had coached me a great deal—so that I knew how I was expected to handle myself, where to aim for with the harpoon, and how to use the lance. He drilled and drilled me so that while it was my first appearance on any stage as a devil-fisher, I was by no means ignorant of the art.

"On the second fish we struck, Coles's iron pulled out. He got it a second time. This one towed us two miles.

"One of our specimens when we came to measure it proved to be the second largest of which there is any record of being killed. Coles has the record fish.

"We did not have such good luck on the second day, the one fish we struck being lost. In this respect it is like every other kind of sport; you must figure on having good luck and bad, and on days when you will get nothing as well as the rare days when you will get a big bag."

"You call this fish the 'big game of the sea.' How does it compare with big-game killing ashore," I asked.

"It is difficult of comparison because all of the circumstances are so different. Both are good, but I think I prefer the land game. I am too much of a landlubber not to have a preference for solid earth under my feet. But it is great sport, and I am going back when I have more time to spare, just as I hope to get another chance at lions in Africa. I have no desire for the bigger game, elephants and that sort of thing, but I would like a few more lions.

"Like all big-game hunting, in devil-fishing you have to depend very much on your guides, and you must expect some considerable danger of being hurt. The fish will not attack any-one, but when attacked they will fight back. At the risk of being called a nature faker I'll add that the male of the species has been known to attack a boat which has been made fast to a female. At least, that is what veterans of the sport tell. Like everything else of the sort, this is something one would have to verify. However, Coles, who like most scientists is skeptical of many things, is inclined to credit these stories.

"Coles, by the way, got into this thing in a rather unusual way. He had the groundwork of a good education when he went into devil-fishing and shark-hunting because he had become wearied of other fishing. The scientific side of the thing appealed to him, and when he began to look things up, he found that very little work had been done. Now he is probably the world's best authority in this line. He has also gone to the point where he made shark fishing attractive from a commercial standpoint. He has no interest in the commercial side of the thing—he has passed that up to others after spending quite a lot of money in pioneer work. That, of course, is the scientist of it."

Colonel Roosevelt's last college degree—that Doctor of Science—was awarded to him by Trinity College, at the same time Coles received a similar honor. To be invested in the degree they journeyed together to Hartford. On their return, the colonel said he had had a "bully" time.[9]

TEACHING "THE LITTLE FELLOW" HOW TO FISH

In 1926, Calvin Coolidge had the temerity to tell a press conference that fishing was a waste of time and worthwhile only for old men and small boys. Maybe Coolidge had already decided not to run and so didn't care about the storm of outrage that followed. But his Secret Service chief, Colonel Edmund Starling, did and decided to take action. He was himself an avid fly-fisherman and also a bit of a gambler.

I proceeded carefully, for I had made bets with most of the White House staff and some of the Cabinet members, and I did not want to lose. They said I would never get him into a boat or get a fishing rod into his hand.

The Coolidges went to Lake Osgood in the Adirondacks, and in the first few days he would stand on the dock at the boathouse or on the bridge across the bay leading to the residence, and I would get into the guide boat and stand up to cast, demonstrating that the craft was safe and steady and in no danger of turning over. After I hooked a few fish he showed interest. I would put them on the line and show them to him when I came in. Finally, when I had almost begun to lose hope, he said to me one morning, "I'd like to fish this afternoon."

It was not a particularly good day—breezy, with ripples on the lake and a little bright. I had to decide between giving him a nickel-plated Colorado spinner or a copper spinner. I finally decided to let him use a copper spinner, giving it a rub on the sleeve of my hunting coat to make it brighter. Oscar Otis, the superintendent of the estate, handled the boat. The President sat in the middle seat. I was forward. We proceeded along the shore about fifteen feet from the bank.

Nothing happened for the first half hour. Then the President's spinner began to move along near the bank. His line went tight. It was a good-sized fish.

"What'll I do with it?" he yelled at me.

"Keep a taut line with the rod tip up and let him stay in the water," I said.

I motioned to Otis to pull the boat out into open water, away from the shore, so that there would be no interruption in the battle. The President followed my instructions, and in about twenty minutes he had his fish alongside the boat. By this time he was wild with excitement.

"Get him in the boat! Get him in the boat!" he shouted to me.

"He's still your fish," I said, handing him the gaff. "Lift him into the boat with this."

He did but not as I meant. Instead of aiming for one of the gills, he hooked the fish dead center and with a tremendous heave jerked him into the boat. I covered my eyes with my hands. When I was able to look I saw a beautiful Northern pike flopping on the bottom of the boat. The little fellow was sitting down, shaking all over. I winked at Otis and motioned to him to head back to the boathouse.

The pike, which weighed six pounds, I put on a fish string. When we landed, I turned it over to the President, who took it on both hands and hurried up the path to the house. As he approached the cabin, he called loudly for Mrs. Coolidge. She came out on the porch to see what was up. Waving the fish at her, the little fellow cried: "Mama! Mama! Look what I've caught!"

Thereafter we fished every day, rain or shine. The conversion was complete. The little fellow became one of the most ardent fishermen I have ever known, and I collected all my bets.[10]

HERBERT HOOVER: FISHING INTO HIS EIGHTIES

Herbert Hoover fished all his life in both fresh and salt water. He caught salmon and trout and marlin and sailfish. Long after he left the White House, he began going to Florida for bonefishing. He became quite an expert, although he had a few quirks, as one guide, Donald Bowers, observed:

> We'd be poling along, and when you'd see a fish you would have to be fairly quiet—and all of a sudden we'd hear this knock, knock, knock on the side of the boat. Of course, the fish heard it, too. But not knowing the fish was close, why he was cleaning out his pipe. Sometimes it goofed it up, but we learned to live with it.

Another guide, Calvin Albury, fished with Hoover for fourteen years off Key Largo. According to Albury, Hoover was the best bonefisherman he had ever seen. When he first came down to fish, he was dressed in a business suit, necktie, and cuff links, and Albury admitted to some skepticism. "But it didn't take long for him to prove to me how good he was at fishing. I fished with him as many as thirty days in a straight run."

One year, over the span of twenty days, Hoover landed 196 fish that ran from eight to eleven pounds, Albury recalled. "And Mr. Hoover landed more doubleheaders—two at the same time—than any other fifty people that have ever been fishing," he said.

One reason for that was that Hoover had a distinctive way of hooking the fish. "He'd take this line in his hands—he didn't depend on feeling that fish from the tip of the rod—he held that line in his hand, and the minute that fish touched that bait he knew it. He didn't have to wait for a pull of the tip of a rod."

According to Albury, Hoover had a saying: "When a fish strikes, then you strike back; when the fish runs, you rest; and when the fish quits

Hoover in Florida with granddaughter and guide Calvin Albury (on Hoover's right).
HOOVER PRESIDENTIAL LIBRARY.

running, then you go to work." Albury recalled that Hoover always carried
a pack of Life Savers and "when the fishing would be slow, he'd say, "Well,
we'll take a pill and see what happens. . . .""

Generally patient and even-tempered, Hoover once did get livid when
he and Albury were fishing off Homestead air force base in 1950. The
Korean War had broken out and the air force had reactivated the base.
With a tremendous roar, a fighter suddenly came in very low over the pair
in their fishing boat, and trailed jet fumes and soot all over the men's
clothes. Albury recalled, "Mr. Hoover sat there for about three or four
minutes, and he never said a word. Finally he turned around to me and he

said, 'I wish he'd stick that flying blowtorch so far in this mud flat that it would take them twenty-five years to find it.'"

In April 1962, when Hoover was eighty-six years old, he went fishing with Albury.

> When he came in, I had a feeling that this was the last he was going to come down here. That day he took his own wristwatch off his arm, the one that he had been wearing from the time he and I had fished together. And he gave me [this and] his rod and reel and he said, "Here's a little memento for you." He told me, "If I ever get back, I'll use the rod and reel; if I never get back, it's yours. You keep it and do whatever you want with it."[11]

Hoover never came back.

COMPETING FOR THE CATCH

FDR always fished with company because he had to. He fished in all kinds of venues—up and down the Atlantic coast, on the Gulf of Mexico, off California, Panama, to the Galapagos Islands, Nova Scotia, and Ontario. He would troll for hours, and when he tired of that there was always bottom fishing.

Not only did he like to catch fish, he also liked to make the fishing competitive. On the three-week trip to the Galapagos Islands in 1938, with aides Basil O'Connor, Steve Early, and Edwin Watson, among others, the log melodramatically described contests for largest and most fish, heated arguments about fishing methods, and a wordy war over whether a "dehydrated" shark weighing 120 pounds was bigger than a sailfish of 130 pounds.

After one day in which sharks played havoc with food fish and tackle, the party argued long about whether the beast was really a fish and could therefore be counted in the day's catch. All agreed that it was not edible. Perhaps because he had caught a sixty-pounder that day, FDR finally announced that now and henceforth sharks would be numbered among the day's take.[12]

FDR AND I, BY BARNEY FARLEY

"I believe I knew President Franklin Delano Roosevelt as well as anyone, and better than millions of others, even including some of his cabinet members." With that modest statement, Barney Farley—unrelated to James

FDR, his military aide Lt. Col. Edwin Watson, and Secretary of the Interior Harold Ickes josh one another about their respective catches on a cruise aboard the USS Houston in October 1935. FRANKLIN D. ROOSEVELT LIBRARY.

Farley, FDR's postmaster general—began his account of guiding the President for two days' fishing along the jetties and surf of Port Aransas, Texas, in May 1937.[13]

> I knew him as Mr. Roosevelt the fisherman in khaki clothes, relaxed, happy, eager, enthusiastic, knowing he was among people who loved him. He put himself on the same level as others, desirous of learning the things he didn't know, willing to share his wonderful personality with everyone. He was an attentive listener when others were talking. He was a considerate, thoughtful, and compassionate man.
>
> How do I know these things about the President of the United States? I was his fishing guide and advisor on where, when and how to catch fish of his choice and the kind of tackle to use to get the most pleasure while fishing. He believed in my capabilities and judgement when I suggested the approach to the problems that came up that would affect his and his guests' pleasure and comfort, knowing I was vitally interested in the success of his vacation trip.

Farley got the job because he had guided for FDR's son Elliott the year before, and Elliott had had such a good time that he persuaded his father to go to Texas to fish.

In his account of the expedition, Farley missed no opportunity to show his devotion and insight. He gushed as he told how he prevailed upon Roosevelt to use Farley's own rod, how he persuaded the Secret Service to let the President fish in Farley's boat rather than the *Potomac's* launch, how he urged the Secret Service to back off because they were scaring the fish. Once the President started fishing, "[h]e was an apt pupil and did the right things at the right time."

Alas, Roosevelt lost the first tarpon he hooked when it threw the hook as it was about to be boated. On the second day they caught no fish until almost the last minute, when Roosevelt hooked what the party thought was a rock. It turned out to be a fine tarpon. Farley said all the boats surrounding the President stopped fishing just to watch the First Angler.

> Every boat that had been fishing where we were had quit fishing and followed us, taking many pictures, but keeping a respectful distance from our tarpon. We fought this tarpon easy, taking no chances on a broken line. Several times the President had nice things to say about the tackle I had given him. We fought the tarpon over a distance of three and one half miles and one hour and twenty minutes before bringing it to gaff near the lighthouse. Boats closed in on us, everyone congratulating the President and him enjoying the conversation as one fisherman to another. He had learned to fish and handle tackle well and was proud of his capabilities. He reached over and patted the fish on the back and said, "Thanks old fellow, you put up a good fight."

Quite another perspective comes from the man who piloted the boat that day. According to Ted Mathews, there was no titanic battle between noble fisherman and noble fish. It was more like Achilles dragging the body of Hector around the walls of Troy. "Once the fish was hooked, Elliott and Barney demanded that we pull the fish all around the jetties so that people and press could see and take pictures of it. I felt sorry for the President—he never really got a chance to fight that fish."[14]

Barney Farley, a fishing guide in Port Aransas, Texas, displays the tarpon FDR hooked in May 1937 while boat captain Ted Mathews and Elliott Roosevelt look on. AP/WIDE WORLD PHOTOS.

TRUMAN, FISHING, AND GAMBLING

Like Roosevelt, Harry Truman turned fishing trips into competitive outings. Unlike Roosevelt, Truman didn't much like to fish, but he was willing to go along on fishing expeditions because it was "customary and the gang wanted to go."

On one occasion, the President went along on one day's fishing with Admiral William Leahy, Rear Admiral Foskett, Judge Sam Rosenman, Charles Ross, Neil Helm, and Captain W. A. Saunders, commander of the Key West submarine base. Their boat caught the largest and the longest fish of the day in the dollar sweepstakes. But they lost out in the most-numerous category when the second boat, led by Clark Clifford, smuggled aboard a petty officer who was the acknowledged fishing champion of the base.[15]

Truman with Fleet Admiral William D. Leahy display some of their catch on a November 1946 trip to the Dry Tortugas in Florida. HARRY S TRUMAN LIBRARY.

On another outing the presidential party broke up into two teams to fish in torpedo retriever boats. Each of the participants had to put up $5.00. Truman ended up the hands-down winner with a sixteen-pound barracuda and a sixteen-pound grouper.[16]

A few days later Truman's aide General Harry Vaughn and Air Force General Charles Landry caught over ninety pounds of fish, including a nineteen-pound grouper. Over lunch, Vaughn jubilantly recounted how the two generals had simultaneous strikes, and as they reeled in the fish the lines formed a V in the water. "Mr. Truman kept on eating in silence. He did not even ask if it were a two-headed fish."[17]

HOOKING A BROTHER

In 1946, Dwight Eisenhower helped launch a second, more pacific, invasion: a fraternal fishing trip. Instead of being supreme commander, he had to share the decisions with his four brothers, Arthur, Earl, Edgar, and Milton. At first they could not even agree on the place to go. Edgar argued for trout fishing in Washington, Dwight lobbied for the Maryland mountains,

All five Eisenhower brothers gathered in northern Wisconsin for a joint fishing trip in July 1946. Ike demonstrates a no-nonsense style as he casts for muskies, while Arthur (left) watches his lure. REPRINTED WITH THE PERMISSION OF THE *MILWAUKEE JOURNAL SENTINEL.*

Arthur and Earl wanted to go bass fishing in Missouri, and Milton held out for the muskies and walleyes of northern Wisconsin. Milton was the most persuasive, for the five brothers chose Lambert's Deer Farm in Minocqua, Wisconsin, for their weeklong stay.

The expedition was successful in that all brothers caught plenty of fish, and there was lively competition each day for first fish, most fish, and biggest fish. They played practical jokes on each other, including once when Ike put a muskie plug onto Earl's chair.[18]

GETTING SKUNKED WITH IKE
Ten years later, Sunday columnist and Vermont Superior Court judge Milford K. Smith told his readers how a fishless outing could still be sublime when his companion was Dwight Eisenhower, who visited Vermont in June 1955.

The brothers loved playing practical jokes on one another. On the first night, Dwight put a large muskie plug on Earl's chair. The result was unanimous laughter from Arthur through Milton, Earl, and Dwight to Edgar. EISENHOWER PRESIDENTIAL LIBRARY.

Well, you know how it is when you plan to show a friend some wonderful fishing. How, of course, that's the day the fish just won't look at anything. How, even if you know the water is loaded with fish, they just won't cooperate. Well, that's the way it was.

We should have known, and we did, that trout just don't give a hoot who is fishing for them. But we hoped and prayed that even trout might be impressed by a President of the United States. But outside of a few young starvelings who were returned to the brook with a distinction few trout have had of being gently handled by a President, it was pretty much a blank as far as fish were concerned.

Not that the trout were not there. Furnace Brook always has plenty of native trout in its clear waters. But Ben Schley at the Holden Hatchery wasn't taking any chances, and the resident

Eisenhower poses for pre-outing photo with his aide Sherman Adams (left) and Milford K. Smith, a Rutland, Vermont, lawyer and outdoor writer who described fishing with the President. PHOTO BY ALDO MERUSI OF THE *RUTLAND HERALD.*

fish population had been increased by the addition of a good many outsiders. It didn't make any difference. Hatchery trout and native combined in a conspiracy of not hitting.

Now, it's possible we could have caught trout on bait or spinner. But the President of the United States likes to take his trout on feathers or not at all. And he had taken a licking before, and said so. If he hadn't been President of the United States with a timetable of appointments that had to be met he would have been right out there the next morning to see if they could lick him again. He said that, too, and there was a real yearning in his voice.

Because the President is a fisherman and a good one, too. That little two and a half ounce bamboo did just what it was supposed to do in his hands. The light leader glistened over the water, and the Spirit of Pittsford Mills, famed fly of the

Furnace, settled in just the tiny pocket of water that it was intended to reach. Of course, an alder branch would now and then seize his fly in the same exasperating manner that alder bushes have with the flies of less noted anglers. But there was no savage yank that marks the impatient and inexperienced fisherman, resulting in broken leader and lost fly. Sure, there might have been a remark under the breath, but the fly was released with careful hands and the fishing resumed.

Most sportsmen, because they are sportsmen, know that all there is of fishing is not the catching of fish. The sparkling clarity of a mountain stream, a view of distant hills through an opening in the trees, the flash of a disturbed bird, all are part of their fishing enjoyment. We said that the President was a fisherman, and it's high time we added that he is a sportsman. Every detail of the setting in which he fished registered itself upon his senses and received its comment; a stand of birches gleaming in their whiteness against the dark of the evergreens, a hawk circling in the hot sky, even the caddis nymphs dislodged from their rocky homes by boot-shod feet.

What did we talk about? Well, you know what fishermen talk about. Flies and leaders and reels and rods. Water that we have fished and waters that we hope to fish. Big trout that we caught, and bigger trout that we didn't. Which takes a dry fly more readily, a rainbow or brown trout. Felt soles on waders as compared to hobnails. Whether or not wings on a dry fly are necessary. All those wonderful and useless things that are so much nonsense to the non-fisherman but are meat and drink to the dedicated angler.

Did he have a good time? Well, he is the only one who could answer that question, although there were certain incidents that would indicate that he did. A man doesn't go without lunch to fish for an extra hour, ordinarily, if he isn't having a good time. Especially when he says he'd rather fish than eat and only has time for a sandwich on returning before setting off again in that big silver plane. Or hums to himself a little while expertly placing a fly on the edge of the fast white water. Or says that it's the most relaxing time he has had in many long months.

What's it like fishing with a President? Well, we don't know about other Presidents. It isn't too often that our fishing companions hold such exalted stations in life. But fishing with this President, Dwight D. Eisenhower, is like fishing with your best friend, taking it for granted that this friend of yours is as fine an angler, sportsman and gentleman as you ever knew.[19]

Trying to make sure that Ike caught fish, eager beavers at the U.S. Fish Hatchery in nearby Pittsford stayed up past midnight hauling fat two-to three-pound rainbows from the pools to Furnace Brook. Unfortunately, the change of environment was too much of a shock for the fish, and they refused to strike any of the flies Ike cast at them. As Harold Blaisdell, one who helped in the stocking, wrote later, "It can be added that local fishermen fared considerably better after the big trout had been at least partially acclimated. Unaware of the nocturnal stocking, and prepared for fish only a few inches over the legal length limit, these fishermen left the stream in a happy daze, toting trout that wouldn't fit in their creels."[20]

JIMMY CARTER SHARES HIS FLIES

A number of times in his memoir *An Outdoor Journal,* Jimmy Carter mentions the pleasure he got in tying his own flies and then catching fish on them. Perhaps an even greater delight derived from sharing those flies with other fishermen when they were getting skunked. On a six-hour stopover in Alaska to fish for grayling, Carter described this joy.

We finally landed on a small body of water known as Clarence Lake. Wading out into the extremely cold water for a few yards, we placed our flies as far out as possible, let them sink for twenty or thirty seconds, and then reeled in slowly as the fly conformed to the steep underwater slope. Although I was relatively inexperienced at fly-fishing with sinking tip lines and my casts were shorter than most of the others, I had one small fly I'd created that seemed to be exceptionally attractive to the grayling. It was an imitation of a small yellow caterpillar, tied with a chenille body and peacock herl strips down the back, and it worked when nothing else would. That was a proud moment for me, as a novice fly-tyer, when I shared my creation with the other more experienced anglers.[21]

Don't let anyone kid you. This huge tarpon was caught by Florence Harding, while the President had to settle for one only 4 feet 9 inches long. PHOTO BY ROBERT RUNYON, THE CENTER FOR AMERICAN HISTORY, THE UNIVERSITY OF TEXAS AT AUSTIN.

PRESIDENTIAL FISHING WIVES

Presidential fishing is generally a male preserve. But there are quite a few tantalizing nibbles about the wives who have fished. Charles Francis Adams tells how he delighted in fishing with his mother, the wife of John Quincy Adams. As a girl, Julia Grant loved to go fishing and wrote in her memoirs: "Oh! what happiness to feel the pull, and to see the plunge of the cork; then the little quivering, shining creature was landed high on the bank."[22]

Austine Snead, whose pen name was Miss Grundy, was a gossip columnist for the *New York Daily Graphic* and a friend of President Rutherford Hayes. She wrote on May 26, 1878:

> Mrs. Hayes is greatly enjoying the trout fishing in the Adirondacks. She is especially fond of fishing. She and the Vice-President and their party are living in the woods, but not in tents. They telegraphed last week giving the weight of a fish caught by one of their number, which was so prodigious that

According to the family photographer, Bess Truman was a more enthusiastic angler than Harry, but in this photo from a trip to Florida, he seems to be having more fun. HARRY S TRUMAN LIBRARY.

the President and his niece thought the telegraphic operator must have made a mistake, and telegraphed back to know if such a catch had really been made. . . .[23]

The Hayeses' only daughter, Fanny, once observed that her father did little fishing. "As to his two hobbies being fishing and chess in that order, I cannot remember that he emulated Izaak Walton in any manner. On the other hand, my mother was a devoted fisherman—and I used to say she would fish from sunup to sunset whether she caught anything or not!"[24]

A week after Warren Harding's election in 1920, on a fishing vacation in Texas, Harding watched as his wife, Florence, caught a bigger tarpon than he had. She had been fishing along the surf in a small boat with Senator Frederick Hale of Maine when the tarpon took her mullet. For a quarter of an hour she gamely hung on while the fish raced back and forth along the beach. Then Hale took the rod and brought it to gaff. The

George and Barbara Bush share the pride of their catch. GEORGE BUSH PRESIDENTIAL LIBRARY.

tarpon was five feet nine inches long, weighed over two hundred pounds, and was, according to the locals, the largest one caught that season. Mrs. Harding decided to have it stuffed.[25]

Grace Coolidge learned to fish and, unlike her husband, was willing to bait her own hook. According to the *New York Times,* Mrs. Coolidge fished in the rain, waded the stream, and ducked under trees "like a regular nimrod." On her first day she caught a nine-inch rainbow and ordered it cooked for the President's dinner.[26]

According to family photographer Ken White, Bess Truman was a much more enthusiastic angler than Harry. "She loved to fish. She wouldn't do it in public much. If people knew about it, they would crowd around, and that made her nervous. During their courting days, she fished a lot. When they went to Key West, she fished occasionally."

On occasion, Barbara Bush fished with George.[27]

But Rosalynn Carter was (and is) in a class by herself. According to Jimmy, the two began fishing together when he was governor of Georgia.

> She had a knack for the sport and liked it, especially the soli-
> tude and beauty of the woodlands. She first tried fly-fishing in
> August 1978, on a raft trip down the Middle Fork of Idaho's

In the early days of their shared love of fly-fishing, Rosalynn and Jimmy would go out to practice on ponds near their farm in Plains, Georgia (1978). JIMMY CARTER LIBRARY.

River of No Return. . . . And on the Snake River and the shore of Jackson Lake in Grand Teton National Park. Rosalynn soon developed a very delicate presentation which, on short casts, was especially effective with trout. Her skills developed even further during our presidential visits to Spruce Creek. Through it all, however, she relished being by herself, almost always within sight of me and others but far enough away to do her own thing. It was disturbing to me how many times she caught the largest or the most trout, leaving me to equal her catches only by rising earlier and fishing longer![28]

For the Carters, fishing was not only a way to get away from the demands of office and supplicants but also a way to be together. These short fishing outings were "squeezed into the interstices of a busy presidential life. They were always too brief but especially welcome. For a few hours we enjoyed the solitude we badly needed."[29]

As they became more adept, the Carters fished often at Wayne Harpster's farm on Spruce Creek in Pennsylvania (October 1980). JIMMY CARTER LIBRARY.

One place they loved to go was the Pennsylvania farm of Wayne Harpster, who leased land to the Spruce Creek Hunting and Fishing Club. Over a dozen times, the Carters helicoptered to Harpster's place for overnight or weekend stays.

According to Harpster, "Rosalynn became quite a good fisherman. I thought there were times when she caught on quicker than he did because he was preoccupied with other things. I spent a lot of time with her."[30]

Modest about his own teaching talents, Harpster then brought in Professor George Harvey of Pennsylvania State University to teach the Carters. "She learned more quickly than almost anyone I ever taught to cast. One day I taught her the slack leader cast and then took her to a pool where she caught over twenty fish and never moved from one spot. I netted and released all the trout for her. She turned the pool over to her son Chip, and he couldn't catch any."[31]

As Mrs. Carter recalled,

At first, it was a horrible experience to have someone there watching me make all those mistakes. But I worked hard at it. Then I would take all these instructions from George and go back and spend hours and hours casting in the swimming pool at Camp David.

Fly-fishing is so different from just sitting in a boat. When you're out fishing, it totally clears my mind. I don't think about work or anything that is pressing. There's no doubt that one of the reasons you are relaxed is that you become so focused on all the things of fishing. It's so different from being in public and being conscious of all the people around you. To me it's also a challenge to try to cast where I want to cast and to get the fly to land exactly where I want it to land. It's also a wonderful time to be outdoors with nature. Indeed, some of the best times of my life have been fishing with Jimmy. As Jimmy and I "leap-frog" up a stream, we never get out of sight. We don't talk much. Occasionally, if he is catching fish on a particular fly, he will tell me or vice versa.

Spruce Creek was a wonderful escape for us. When you are in the White House, you are so busy and there are so many decisions you have to make every single day, and being with people all the time . . . we could go to Spruce Creek, and not have to dress up and just be refreshed by the experience.

We did have to teach the Secret Service not to "advance" the stream and spoil the fishing by walking right down to the bank and scaring the fish.

And the best part was that the press never found out. Our routine was to helicopter to Camp David on Friday afternoons and land. The press always had to be there for landings and take-offs. Then they would go into the little town nearby and stay until we were scheduled to go back to the White House on Sundays. When we were going to Spruce Creek, we would wait until the press left, then get back in the helicopter and fly over to Wayne's, land in the pasture, and fish. We would be sure to be back at Camp David early on Sundays. The press never knew we were gone. It was absolutely wonderful. We could go and be normal people. It was so great for us because we didn't get that kind of escape very often. When we were fishing, we were not public property.

I would recommend fly-fishing to anyone in public service who wants to stay sane![32]

The Carters still go to Spruce Creek nearly every year, and they take their fly rods almost every time they travel abroad.

STREAMSIDE SURGERY

Don Daughenbaugh has fished with Jimmy Carter for over twenty years. One of his early memories involves an emergency. The memorable incident occurred on a trip to the Snake River in Wyoming in 1978:

> It was a cool, sunny day in August. There was a strong wind blowing into President Carter's face. While he was casting a #10 Red Humpy upstream to a nice Snake River cutthroat, and being in a hurry because he had already caught a few, a crosswind caught his back cast and imbedded the hook deeply in his cheek. Dr. [William] Lukash, his personal physician, quickly put him down on the riverbank and began pulling the hook from his cheek. It was painful, but the President did not move a muscle or show signs of distress. After several minutes and no success, I reluctantly instructed the doctor to use our tried-and-true leader method. The problem was readily solved. I was impressed with the President's endurance and the fact that all he wanted was a closeup photo of the fly sticking in his cheek. I will always remember how quickly he got back to fishing for the cutthroats. Afterwards Dr. Lukash said, "I have read about that method and tried it on an orange but never tried it on a human. Sure glad you were here. It really works."[33]

BUSH'S BLUE-COLLAR BUDDY, BOILARD

Bob Boilard is George Bush's age, a stocky round-faced man with a ready smile. He was born in Biddeford, Maine, on the Saco River. At the age of eighteen he joined the U.S. Marine Corps Air Corps and spent the war as an aircraft mechanic in the South Pacific. He returned home to get a job as a machinist in the shipyards of Portsmouth, New Hampshire, and Kittery, Maine, and retired with the rank of metals inspector. Along the way he established a fishing guide service for striped bass and bluefish that was so successful his business cards promised "No Fish, No Pay." For years he has been a vocal member and co-founder of the Saco (River) Corridor

George Bush and his buddy Bob Boilard share their bluefish off Kennebunkport, Maine.
GEORGE BUSH PRESIDENTIAL LIBRARY.

Commission, which seeks to preserve that drainage basin from public and private pollution.[34]

According to Boilard, his first meeting with Bush took place—where else?—out on the water:

> In 1983, I was fishing for bluefish near Wood Island Lighthouse eight miles off Walker's Point, and I was catching them pretty good. Suddenly I heard a voice yelling, "What are you catching them on?" I looked around and I saw this flotilla of boats—Secret Service, the Coast Guard, press, onlookers—and there was the Vice President, George Bush, in his boat *Fidelity.*
>
> I told him it was a Rebel popping plug. He said he was using a Rebel swimming plug but not catching anything. Well, he switched to the popping plug. Then, I told him to turn his boat around and follow me. In less than two hundred feet he got two bluefish on, and I had one. He got so excited, he says, "Sometime I want to go fishing with you. Give me your telephone number." Then he gives me his number! "I'm on vacation. Keep me abreast of area action. Call me any time!"

After the Secret Service checked me out, I got a call to go
fishing, and we've been fishing ever since.

In all, Boilard has fished with Bush over a score of times. Among the
other guests on those Boilard-guided outings were the Reverend Billy
Graham, a Portuguese prime minister, and French President Mitterand's
security chief. Boilard has never asked for money. "I told him I came out
of retirement to fish with him. He gave me a pair of daggers once—said
they would be good for cleaning fish with."

When he was fishing, Bush could be impatient, Boilard noted. "Several times, we would be fishing and he would see someone else catching a
fish, and he'd want to race over there to join in. And I would have to say,
'The fish are everywhere; *fish here!*' And usually when we waited, we'd
catch fish. When we first fished together, he wanted to use this light bass-
casting rod and eight-pound-test line! Imagine that—he wanted to use that
little six-foot buggy whip on a ten-to fifteen-pound bluefish. 'Mr. Vice
President,' I said, 'when you go for whales you have to use whale equipment.' "

The pair never talked politics. "The world's problems I leave to him.
On his vacation, he wants to fish. When we do talk, it's mostly family, fishing memories, and fishing prospects. Sometimes the President would ask
about things going on in Maine, and I told him. He could have helped us a
lot to save the Saco River. But we never asked him for that."

Did Bush ever complain about the intrusions on his fishing?

"He wasn't a complainer. When we would go out, in no time there
were lots of boats. I don't know if they smelled him or passed it out by
radio. But he would wave to them. He'd say, 'Those people are having fun,
too.' "

During the vice-presidential years, Boilard would spend time going
through Bush's equipment, replacing worn-out hooks or broken lures and
putting on new line. On their trips together, he made Bush the chief "field
tester" of his experiemental lures, often cobbled together with odd pieces
of hardware, dime-store spoons, and such things as hair from a Miss Piggy
Halloween mask.

Within a few months of his victory in 1988, Bush returned the favor.
Among the hundreds of appointments Bush made in his administration was
one that did not require senatorial approval. On White House stationery,
in Bush's own writing, the new President declared that Bob Boilard was
now "Master of Tackle Boxes."

GEORGE BUSH AND THE RAPALA EARRING

George Bush invited many political leaders to visit him at Kennebunkport, but not many ventured out to fish with the President. Prime Minister Brian Mulroney of Canada was one who did. Bush's son Jeb accompanied the two heads of state. According to the President:

> It was dead calm and a perfect day for bluefish. You could see them coming in chasing the mackerel, trashing them. We were casting with spinning rods and Rapalas or bait and catching fish. Now, the bail was not working well on Jebby's reel, and he had a bad cast and it came winging back and pierced my ear so that the barb went right through the ear.
>
> There I was with this big Rapala plug hanging from my ear. Mulroney said, "Gosh, we'd better go in and get that attended to." But I said, "Jeez, we don't get fishing like this very often; we're not going in now."
>
> So, Jerry, one of the Secret Service men, pulled out some clippers, cut off the barb, and pulled the hook back through the ear, and we kept on fishing, catching a lot of fish. It was one of the greatest bluefishing days I have seen up here.
>
> If that had been in the eyeball, I guess we would have gone in, but it wasn't and we didn't.[35]

CHAPTER TEN

AFFECTATIONS AND PRETENSES

Shall I use the whole worm?   *—Calvin Coolidge to a Wisconsin guide*

I don't use worms. I want fishing to be a challenge.   *—Dwight Eisenhower*

I was piscatorially retarded. . . .   *—Jimmy Carter*

A ll men are equal before fish" observed Herbert Hoover. But are all fish equal before men? As fly-fishing historian Paul Schullery wrote: "Even the most open-minded of modern anglers speak of having 'graduated' from baitfishing to fly fishing, of having passed through an important, educational youthful phase as a 'worm drowner' or 'hardware flinger.' "[1] Hoover described fishing's class structure in even greater detail:

> The dry-fly devotees hold themselves a bit superior to the wet-fly fishermen; the wet-fly fishermen, superior to the spinner fishermen; and the spinners, superior to the bait fishermen. I have noticed, however, that towards the end of the day when there are no strikes, each social level collapses in turn down the scale until it gets some fish for dinner.
>
> The swordfish and tarpon fishermen have some social distinctions on the basis of the size of line and reel. The lower-thread line operators are the dukes and earls in that aristocracy. The swordfish and marlin devotees are naturally superior to those who take merely mackerel, amberjack, or flounders. The bonefish fishermen claim a little superiority to the tarpon seekers. But it is not the economic status that counts in such good society so much as knowing what the fish bite.[2]

When Herbert Hoover fished, in salt water or fresh, he was invariably dressed in a coat and tie. COURTESY THE AMERICAN MUSEUM OF FLY-FISHING.

One day in July 1927, while on a summer-long vacation in the Black Hills of South Dakota, Calvin Coolidge returned from a day's fishing, pleased as punch. He had caught five trout. (He didn't know that Edmund Starling, his Secret Service chief, had supervised the stocking of hundreds of rainbow and lochleven trout that were penned in by log and wire-mesh booms across the river.) Reporters asked him which fly he had caught them on. No fly, Coolidge said, he had used worms.

Reactions were swift and enraged. "WORMS!" gasped the newspaper headlines. Chapters of the Izaak Walton League denounced his unsportsman-like conduct. Even other politicians jumped on Coolidge. Senator William Borah of Idaho declared that he had never heard of worm fishing for trout. He contended that Coolidge had caught catfish and mistaken them for trout, "but if they were trout, they must have been imbeciles." Senator James Reed of Missouri was equally scornful: "Any trout that will lie on the bottom of a lake and bite a worm is a degenerate trout. As a matter of generosity and common fairness, however, I hope he used a whole worm."[3]

Free at last! "Ding" Darling shows a delighted Coolidge fishing with worms in Wisconsin in the summer of 1928 now that he doesn't have to worry about re-election. In the distance the press chase after the Republican nominees, Herbert Hoover and Charles Curtis of Kansas. COURTESY THE J. N. "DING" DARLING FOUNDATION.

Starling, the common-sensical Secret Service chief, said that the controversy was silly: "Any fisherman will use worms rather than go home with an empty creel."[4]

Thereafter, Coolidge dutifully fished with flies when Starling was watching, but he never lost his affinity for worms. As he told a Wisconsin guide on his Brule River vacation the next year, "I much prefer bait-fishing. I have tried fly-fishing before with about as much success as I'm having here. Herbert Hoover is a special friend of mine, and we've enjoyed fishing together at various times. He is an excellent fly-fisherman and has tried on occasion to teach me his incredible technique." As they fished a stretch of the Brule with little current, Coolidge asked if he should use a sinker. No, said the guide, the weight of the bait alone would pull the hook down.

"Shall I use the whole worm or break it in half?" asked the ever-frugal Coolidge.

"Put on the whole worm . . . and then put on two more. Put on all the worms the hook can possibly hold, being sure to let the ends wiggle."

According to the guide, Coolidge then caught a slew of trout on worms, grasshoppers, and even flies.[5]

Long after Coolidge was dead, writer Frederick Van de Water came to the defense of worms—and perhaps, by extension, to Cal's defense as well, when he wrote,

> With worms you played more fairly with the trout. You offered him what he wanted most. You bet a worm and he wagered himself. If the trout lost, he usually had the worm, or most of it, not just a mouthful of deception to add bitterness to surrender. Fly-fishing, comparatively, was a cheap fraud in which the victim staked his all against an utterly inedible jigger that looked like something it wasn't. The trout could not possibly gain anything; he could lose everything on nothing more estimable than vanity. The sole death-bed comfort he possibly could derive was the knowledge that he had been hooked by a purist. It is easy to understand why a politician might come to prefer flies.[6]

Coolidge's association with worms was so widely known that his successor, Herbert Hoover, while a candidate in 1928, received an indignant letter from a Kentucky businessman, saying,

I will irrespective of politics vote for you if you fish for trout with the fly. But if you use dirty worms like Cal, goodbye.

I enclose two Scotch "Hare-lug" flies, do not trouble returning them if you use worms. I am not like a Scot, when another asked him for a match to light his pipe and then for some tobacco to fill it.

The first replied I hae nae got any so you'll be gaeing me back my match.

I have however four more of these flies if you find them deadly as in Scotland as our bass want a mouthful.

I will just add, knowing your fine record, you will get our votes, fly or worm.[7]

In 1937, then ex-President Herbert Hoover was fishing in the Northwest with O. Glenn Saxon, president of Yale University. The proprietor of a group of cabins where the pair were staying offered them some flies she had tied herself. "I hope you don't use worms like President Coolidge," she said scornfully. Hoover suppressed a smile. "Oh, no, ma'am. I never stoop to such lowdown tactics, but this fellow Saxon here does— and don't give any of your flies to him. He wouldn't appreciate them."[8]

Franklin D. Roosevelt was no piscatorial purist. He had done some fishing as a boy and even some fly-fishing as a young man. After his polio attack, however, Roosevelt could not stand or walk unaided, let alone ply a stream or walk a beach. But within a year of contracting the disease, FDR was fishing again.

He could fish from the back of pleasure boats and from specially constructed seats on naval vessels. Indeed, Roosevelt became an omnivorous saltwater angler. He would fish for tarpon, sailfish, shark, or dogfish. On a fishing expedition to the Galapagos Islands in 1938, Roosevelt's party, which included scientists from the Smithsonian Institution, brought back more than eighty different species of fish. Again in 1941, waiting for Churchill to meet him in Argentia Bay, Nova Scotia, Roosevelt relaxed by fishing. Trolling or bottom fishing, he loved it all.

Such wide-ranging angling didn't immunize him from criticism. Fred Seibel, editorial cartoonist for the *Richmond Times-Dispatch,* made an invidious comparison between what he considered the modest fishing styles of Coolidge and Hoover and the royal treatment given to Roosevelt.

Harry Truman, on the other hand, fished but was not a fisherman. If the political occasion (or the vacation opportunity) called for fishing, he

The Sport of Presidents

Cartoonist Fred Seibel had no sympathy for Roosevelt's handicap as he contrasted the luxury of the President's fishing with the simplicity of his two Republican predecessors.

In this photo taken in Scotland in August 1918, the Assistant Secretary of the Navy Franklin D. Roosevelt takes a break from his fishing and his official duties to ward off the Scottish streamside chill. There is no record of his catch. In fact, it is not clear if the photo was taken before or after Roosevelt's fishing foray. FRANKLIN D. ROOSEVELT LIBRARY.

In this undated photo taken at Warm Springs, Georgia, Roosevelt takes two different comforts simultaneously—a bit of bamboo pole fishing and the company of an unnamed dog. FRANKLIN D. ROOSEVELT LIBRARY.

would dutifully comply. Once, on the Green River in Idaho, he even consented to cast a fly. But he could take fishing or leave it. His old buddy from Kansas City Eddie Jacobson agreed Truman wasn't much of a fisherman. "[H]e always said that the reason he never caught any fish was that he didn't like to eat fish."[9]

Dwight Eisenhower did care about his fishing. After some bait and plug fishing for muskies in northern Wisconsin with his brothers in 1946, he settled into fly-fishing almost exclusively. Fishing with worms was too easy, he thought. As he told a press conference once, "I don't use worms. I want fishing to be a challenge."

Somewhere out there in Cleveland's fishing commonwealth, George Bush and Jimmy Carter passed each other, like ships from different ports. Jimmy Carter grew up in the bass and catfish country of Georgia, and he could have remained a fishing bubba all his life. But he wanted more out of fishing and began trying other forms of angling when he was in the navy. Yet he still described himself as "piscatorially retarded" until he became

Ike fishes at Little Boy Falls on the Magalloway River in Maine on a "nonpolitical" trip to New England in June 1955. The guide is Don Cameron. EISENHOWER PRESIDENTIAL LIBRARY.

governor of Georgia and discovered trout fishing in the frigid waters of the
Chattahoochee River. There he learned the basics from Jack Crockford,
the director of Georgia's Fish and Game Department. His real conversion
occurred while he was President, and in his memoir he described its
appeal:

> Although I had fished for bass, bream, catfish, and other
> warm-water fish since I was a child, and still enjoy it as much as
> ever, there is something special about fly-fishing for trout. By
> taking up this sport fifteen years ago, I entered a world of cold
> and pure flowing waters, rocks and waterfalls, quiet streams
> often nestled in meadows of mint and wild flowers, cool moun-
> tain valleys, personal solitude, and the exquisite science of imi-
> tating and presenting a myriad of sometimes tiny insects that
> comprise the elusive trout's diet. . . .
>
> Fly-fishing at its best includes some of the elements of primal
> hunting; understanding the habitat of the trout, stalking an out-
> standing specimen while concealing your own presence,
> thoughtful assessment of what is always a unique situation, plan-
> ning strategy, and intelligent execution of it with enough
> deception to prevail. Then, perhaps a salute or apology to a
> worthy adversary and—a significant difference the ability to
> release the prey unharmed.[10]

Perhaps it was the engineer in Carter (as in Hoover) that drew the man
to the complex recreation of fly-fishing. Both pursued the fish with passion, diligence, and a commitment to lifelong learning. Carter accumulated
a library of books about trout habits, fly tying, and casting techniques. So
smitten was he with fly-fishing that he told Don Zahner of *Fly Fisherman*
magazine that once at a South Lawn ceremony he had "eyed wantonly a
bushy-tailed squirrel on the lawn—not as a harbinger of Washington spring
but as fodder for his newly installed fly-tying bench" in the room that he
and Harry Truman had both used as an office.[11] In a 1991 interview with
Howell Raines of the *New York Times,* Carter observed,

> It is hard to talk without derogating other kinds of fishing,
> which I also enjoy. But at the same time, fly-fishing to me
> opened up just a new panorama of challenge because you have
> to learn the intricacies of streams, or currents, of water temper-
> ature, of different kinds of fly hatches, how to tie your

Jimmy Carter concentrates on bringing in his fish on the upper Potomac River in September 1980. The election was both six weeks and light years away from Carter. JIMMY CARTER LIBRARY.

Jimmy Carter gets a couple of casting tips from fly-fishing legend Vincent Marinaro. AMERI-
CAN MUSEUM OF FLY-FISHING.

own flies, which you wouldn't ordinarily do in other kinds of fishing.[12]

Raines went on to observe:

Getting out of the White House freed Carter for some notable accomplishments. He took an 8-pound trout that remains a record for the New Zealand lodge where he stayed.

After a spectacular fight, he also took a 12-pound rainbow in Alaska that he describes in his book as the fish of a lifetime.

As a committed catch-and-release fisherman, Carter was troubled by the lodge's decision to kill and mount the fish.

So what about the likeness of his huge Alaska rainbow that is on display above Carter's tying desk?

The former President, who is a stickler for detail, wants to be perfectly clear about one thing. Underneath the speckled fish is this brief signed statement in Carter's block printing:

THIS RAINBOW STILL LIVES. CAUGHT IN THE COPPER RIVER IN WESTERN ALASKA IN JUNE, 1985. HE WAS MEASURED, PHOTOGRAPHED, RELEASED UNHARMED AND REPRODUCED BY A JAPANESE TAXIDERMIST.

If a "class thing" in fishing was really at work, George Herbert Walker Bush, Yale, Skull and Bones, should have learned to make his own flies, to cast for Atlantic salmon in the Miramichi or the Cascapedia. Instead, he cut his teeth (and fingers) on pollack and cod off the rocks of Kennebunkport and fished happily with the bubbas in bass country. In a 1989 interview for *Fly Rod & Reel* magazine, writer Jim Merritt quoted Bush on his own modest, yet various, fishing experiences.

I am not a skilled fly fisherman. This summer on the Shoshone in Wyoming I did pretty well with the dry fly. I got fairly accurate, and I enjoyed the test. The fish were small, but the thrill of laying the fly under a branch and then seeing the fish rise gave me total peace. Mostly I troll for blues (fourteen-pound test and light tackle), spin or bait cast for bonefish and tarpon. I also like bait casting for bass. In Maine, for me it is mostly ten to fifteen pound blues using plugs, bright red or yellow tubing, or Rebel-Rapala-type lures. When the blues are hitting, the type of lure doesn't matter much. A good feather lure or a shiny spoon will do the job. I have had good luck with mackerel going for the blues.

I like catching mackerel on light spinning tackle. I like striped bass fishing but have not starred in this. I've fished a couple of Oregon rivers for steelhead—not much luck. I've fished in Idaho and Alaska, Texas, Alabama, Florida, Maine, and Mexico. Offshore, I like watching the dolphin come across the water. Kings and a hard hitting 'cuda are fun. I have caught sailfish but am not a "big" fish fisherman.[13]

And instead of wading quietly in trout streams, he raced to the fishing grounds in a cigarette boat called *Fidelity.* "You go fast out to where the fish are," he told writer George Plimpton for *Sports Illustrated,* "or [where] you think they are, stop and fish for an hour, and then run for the twenty minutes back. If the sea is up a little, and you're cutting through the waves, well, the combination is just heaven for me."[14]

Yet after leaving office, George Bush has become an enthusiastic, even a fanatical, fly-fisherman. A number of times he has gone fishing for arctic char in several Canadian provinces. When he visited Ft. Simpson, Northwest Territories, Arthur Milnes, a local newspaper editor and self-described "presidential junkie," persuaded Bush to write a column about his fishing. What follows is "The Thrill of Northern Fishing" in the *Deh Cho Drum* for September 4, 1997:

I love fishing the Tree River. Way above the treeline, the fast-flowing Tree River pours its rushing green-gray waters into the Arctic Ocean, about a mile or two from where I fished for char.

As the waters race over the boulders and rocks, you can catch an occasional glimpse of the majestic char, struggling to continue their fight against the current, their quests to reach their destiny, up-river quest.

If thirsty, you can cup your hands and drink of these pristine waters.

Yes, there are some mosquitoes around, but not enough to detract from the joys of fishing. Even a mild breeze seems to keep the critters away.

This year the weather was perfect. We fished in T-shirts, needing a sweater or a jacket only in the early morning or the late afternoon. The weather up there is variable, and it can get very wet and very cold even in August, but not this year.

There were a lot of char in those fast-running waters, a lot of big, strong fish. My 13-year-old grandson, Jeb, from Miami, Fla., got a 25–30-pound fish on his Magog Smelt fly—a brown, wet fly that was very productive over the course of our whole trip.

He fought the fish for 45 minutes, following our guide, Andy's, instructions to perfection. The big red, finally tiring, came into the shallow waters just above some rapids, and then with one ultimate surge of energy, he flipped over the edge of the pool into the white-water rapids, broke the 20-pound test tippet, and swam to freedom.

My grandson, not an experienced fly-fisherman, had fought the fish to perfection. He did nothing wrong. All the fishing experts who were watching told him so, but these big fish are strong and tough and they never give up.

I had 43 fish on my fly rod, only to bring two into the shore. Don't laugh; I was proud to have kept the fly in the water, kept on casting, having the thrill of having that many fish, even for a moment, on my No. 9 rod. I used an L. L. Bean reel.

As for the flies, I found that the Mickey Finn, the Blue Charm, and the Magog Smelt all worked well. So did some others, the names of which escape me even as I write.

I tried some dry flies, but they produced zilch in the way of action.

I found that I got most of my fish on when the fly was drifting down stream, though I got two or three hits the instant the fly hit the water. One pool was narrow, right next to the fast part of the water. I'd throw the fly into the white-capped waves, and it would be rushed by the current into the pool. When it left the raging water and hit the more placid pool, the fish would strike.

I did better on getting the fly unhooked from the rocks this year, though I did lose a tiny number of flies when they were claimed by some especially craggy rocks.

I learned that the way to get lots of fish on the line is to keep the hook in the water. Obvious? Well, maybe, but a lot of fishermen seem to hang out waiting for someone else to catch one before they'd do serious fly fishing.

The rocks were very slick, and, at 73 years of age, my balance is less than perfect. Put it this way: I can't turn very well and I slip a lot. The felt-bottomed boots help. Better still are the felt-bottom boots with little diamond-hard spikes.

I fish a lot, but my advice is, "Get a good guide." I had one in Andy, who in a very gentlemanly way pointed out my mistakes and helped me in every way. He's a good netman, a great fly adviser, and he got as big a kick when I got a fish as if he had taken it himself.

Cartoon of George Bush fishing in the Northwest Territories by Norm Muffit.

Drawing of Grover Cleveland pulling in a bass. CORBIS-BETTMANN.

I find myself getting intolerant of those fishermen using hardware. There is something more sporting, more competitive, more difficult, more challenging about using a fly rod.

I know that the Drum paper is not quite the size of the Toronto papers or the *New York Times*—but you know what? I bet the 800 or 900 readers of your paper know a hell of a lot more about fishing than the readers of those big city papers do.

That made me hesitate about sharing these amateurish observations with you. But, on the other hand, maybe your readers will better be able to sense the exhilarating joy I felt when standing out there knee-deep in the ice-cold waters of the Tree River pools, communing with nature, counting my blessings, thanking God, and catching some char, too.

I'm a very happy and a very lucky man now. Because of time spent fishing and the chance that fishing gives me to relax and [think] freely, now more than ever I see clearly just how blessed

Photo of Grover Cleveland fishing, probably at Tamworth, New Hampshire, in the early 1900s. CORBIS-BETTMANN.

I really am. I served my country. I have a close family and a wonderful wife for 52 and a half years, and, yes, I went to the Tree River and caught char.

Tight lines to all you fishermen![15]

We'll give the final word in this chapter to that passionate but unpretenious angler Grover Cleveland. The danger to fishing's good name, he wrote, lay not only in the excesses of some of its practicioners but in the glorification of one or two breeds of fish.

Bluntly stated, the affectations and pretenses, which I have in mind, and which in my opinion threaten to bring injury upon our noble pursuit, grow out of the undue prominence and exaggerated superiority claimed for fly-casting for trout.[16]

To the sin of pretension, Cleveland added hypocrisy:

> Our irritation is greatly increased when we recall the fact
> that every one of these super-refined fly-casting dictators, when
> he fails to allure trout by his most scientific casts, will chase
> grasshoppers to the point of profuse perspiration, and turn over
> logs and stones with feverish anxiety in quest of worms and
> grubs, if haply [sic] he can with these save himself from empty-
> handedness. Neither his fine theories nor his exclusive faith in
> fly-casting so develops his self-denying heroism that he will turn
> his back upon fat and lazy trout that will not rise.[17]

A proper attitude and generous behavior are all one needs to join the
brotherhood. Common sense plus steadiness and quiet devotion to the
sport are the appropriate virtues for angling, Cleveland believed. Who
holds these in abundance? It is not a boorish underclass. Nor is it a small
self-righteous, self-appointed aristocracy. In the great commonwealth of
fishermen, "It is the middle class in the community of fishermen, those
who fish sensibly and decently . . . upon whom we must depend for the
promotion and protection of the practical interests of the brotherhood."[18]

CHAPTER ELEVEN

MY FAVORITE PRESIDENT

We're cruising down I-89 from Montpelier to Bethel at seventy miles an hour on this June Saturday. My fishing buddy, Syl Stempel, is driving his wife's Subaru. He's drinking a twenty-ounce Coke and talking nonstop about politics, tax cheats, his daughter, women's basketball, and his latest running shoes. A light rain is falling, and you can't see the hillsides for the mist.

Three hours earlier he had called to say that this kind of overcast, drizzly day made for the best fishing on the White River, and did I want to go. Before my wife could say no, I was packed and out the door.

Syl Stempel is the James Carville of the Vermont fishing community—opinionated, passionate, wily, unmovable. He works as hard for the state tax department tracking down out-of-state tax dodgers as he works for Trout Unlimited protecting the state's fishing waters. He's a great fisherman who wastes no money on his outfit and no time on the water. We met when I was in the legislature and he was lobbying for upland stream protection. He catches three fish for every one I hook. I think he takes me along for comic relief.

"OK, Mares, I've listened to you moan about this book for three years. I've been a guinea pig for your prose. It's show time. Which president would you like to fish with?"

"It all depends," I say. "It's like you and me fishing. Sometimes we talk about fishing, and sometimes we talk about politics or life or our kids. It depends upon what I want to get out of the presidents."

"What the hell is that supposed to mean," he grumbles, "what you want out of the presidents?"

"It means, dummy: Are we going to fish or are we going to talk? Do we discuss war and peace and slavery and tariffs and taxes and assault weapons? Or are we going fishing? There's a big difference between the two."

"No kidding!" Syl takes another big swig of Coke.

"Seriously, I've spent three years with these guys, off and on. I feel as if I know some of them pretty well. I even visited Bush, although it was only for an hour. In a way, this whole book is about an activity most of these men could have done without. Political skills were imperative, but being a fisherman? Naw. And yet, I couldn't help thinking that in the course of looking for fishing anecdotes, I read a ton of things about the rest of their public and private lives, one entire book about Roosevelt's handicap, biographies of Washington, Coolidge, and Lincoln. Take Lincoln. I'd love to meet him, but I wouldn't know what to say except thanks. Sure he fished as a kid, like most of them. But as president he was too busy saving the Union."

"Well then, what about the fishing presidents? Which one would you fish with?"

"OK, OK," I say, "but let's be systematic, like you working the water. Let's get rid of the deadwood first—guys like Buchanan and Fillmore and Grant and Johnson (both of them), John Adams—"

"Yeah, yeah, that's easy. I know there were a lot of presidents who didn't fish much."

"You wanted them—Madison, Monroe, Taylor, Tyler, Garfield, Harrison, McKinley, Wilson, Taft, Clinton, your buddy Reagan. . . ." (Syl had been an air-traffic controller who was fired in 1981 during the PATCO strike.)

"Let's talk about the ones who fished," he says, ignoring my jibe. "What about Washington?"

"Now it's getting tougher. Of course, he was a fisherman, and he did some recreational fishing, but his commercial focus makes it harder to find much to say, and, on the patriotic front, I would be almost as tongue-tied with him as with Lincoln. I have a great-great-great grandfather who fought under him, but still I think I would keep my mouth shut."

"Teddy Roosevelt? He was certainly a great outdoorsman."

"Yeah, I like his ranching phase, his exuberance, his trust busting. I'd love to ask him any number of things about his presidency, but he just didn't do much fishing after his youth."

We pull off the highway at Randolph to buy more Coke for Syl and some candy bars and coffee for me and then head back on the road.

"Truman, now there was a good Democrat. You told me he did some fishing."

"Yeah, I think Harry is great. He was tough. He had a great moral compass. He never shirked the big decisions. I'd ask him about the A-bomb, the Berlin Airlift, the Korean War, Joe McCarthy, et cetera. I have a letter from him to my mother. *But* he really didn't fish much, either. Most times he fished, it was out of obligation to his cronies."

"Jeez, Mares, you're harder to nail down than those slime who move to Florida to avoid Vermont income taxes."

"You asked for this. Anyway, I'm just trying to sort it all out in my own head. Let's start talking about presidents who fished and liked it. Well, there's Chester Arthur. He was a Vermonter, if only for two years. He held an Atlantic salmon record up in Canada. Unfortunately, there isn't much else about him except one great story by a New York newspaper reporter named Julian Ralph."

"Coolidge!" Syl exclaims, as he swerves to avoid a dead porcupine. "He was a Vermonter. He fished. We're within spitting distance of Plymouth Notch where he grew up. He's got to be high on your list!"

"Sure, I've got lots of stories about Coolidge. He probably did like to fish, although many of those stories paint him as a cheap and tight-lipped jerk. He only fished with flies under duress. I don't think we'd have much in common."

"Yes, you do—you don't catch many fish! How about Hoover? There's a lifelong fisherman."

"True," I concede. "Among the presidents he was the most direct descendant of Izaak Walton. He wrote some wonderful things about fishing, like it's a long time between bites and so on. But how could you avoid the Depression? If you wanted to talk, it would be like fishing with a mortician."

"OK then, FDR?" asks Syl. "Conqueror of Hoover, author of the New Deal. Great Democrat. I know he fished widely, despite his polio."

"I considered FDR. His was the first direct presidential fishing anecdote I ever had. When I was a kid growing up in Texas, my dad used to take me and my brothers down to Port Aransas to fish. And there in the hotel we always stayed in was a picture of him and a framed, signed tarpon scale taken from a tarpon he caught in May of 1937. But he rarely fished on streams; his polio kept him seated. What's more, one never fished only with him. He always had a gang and a gaggle of aides. And he played everyone off against one another."

"Mares, you're making this hard. It's Carter, then? Here's a guy who got fly-fishing religion in the White House. He worked at the craft. He tied his own flies. He wrote a book about his outdoor experience. He has been a big supporter of Trout Unlimited and the Federation of Fly-Fishers."

"I know, I know," I say. "He did almost as much for fly-fishing as Norman MacLean and Robert Redford did with *A River Runs Through It*. There's a certain finality to his writings on fishing that doesn't invite much conversation. And I confess that I am envious of all the places he gets to fish just because he is an ex-president."

"Agggggh!!! You're not leading up to Bush!?" Stempel turns and looks at me with his most scornful Democratic look.

"Well, he did let me come over to interview him. He's started to do a lot of fly-fishing. He's lent his name to a bonefishing tournament to benefit the Everglades. . . ." I try to think of some other compliments for Bush, which would needle Stempel.

"Mares, if he's your man, you're walking the rest of the way to the White!"

I'm enjoying this. For once, I have his goat. "Come on, Syl, cool down."

"Well, you've dismissed them all as far as I can tell. Who's left?"

"Grover Cleveland, you yo-yo. Haven't I quoted him ad nauseam? Isn't he a Democrat? Didn't he fish all his life?"

"Tell me more," says the dubious Syl.

"Where Hoover was a philosophical fisherman and Carter was a technical fisherman, Cleveland was a psychologist of fishing—with his tongue lodged firmly in his cheek. For every fishing circumstance and attitude, he had something to say—getting skunked, lying, pretensions, bad manners, patience. I love him for his prose, the way he put words together, in that combination of Augustinian confession and Supreme Court brief. He fished with no letup but was understanding of the sport's passing delights. With warmth and wit, Cleveland summed up all that is good and true in fishing."

Stempel is uncharacteristically quiet.

Cleveland quietly working on his gear. PRINCETON UNIVERSITY LIBRARY.

"Shall I go on? I'll go on. As a president, his most salient quality was honesty—in an era of Tammany Hall and the robber barons and the spoils system. He owned up to his paternity of an illegitimate child, which may not even have been his. He showed great physical courage when he had half his jaw removed in a secret cancer operation. He fought his own party on the tariff and the gold standard. That same stubbornness showed up in his fishing, too. We know from editor Richard Gilder that Cleveland would fish through storm and rain. Arguably, he was the most decent, best president among the sad lot who sat in the White House in the last third of the nineteenth century."

"Yeah, but who knows about him? Most people think he was a baseball player."

"That's Grover Cleveland Alexander! Hey, it's my job to teach about him. Cleveland denounced the fishing pretensions of those who would substitute equipment for skill or trumpet flies over bait. He defended the black bass over the trout and salmon. Cleveland made a fisherman's lies respectable, even honorable. 'Our maxim is—in the essentials, truthfulness, in the non-essentials, reciprocal latitude.' How great a one-liner is that? When people don't believe our stories, we can say, as Cleveland did, their believing apparatuses are not properly adjusted."

"I don't lie!" Syl says huffily.

I ignore him. Now I'm in the groove.

"He could defend our sport against public criticism as nothing more serious than gnat stings on the bank of a stream: 'vexations to be borne with patience and afterward easily submerged in the memory of abundant delightful accompaniments.' You see all those pretentious, thoughtless people filling our streams in their designer waders and five-hundred-dollar rods? Listen to what Cleveland says:

> [The true fisherman is] sound at heart. He may not fish well, but if he does not deliberately rush ahead of all companions to pre-empt every promising place on the stream, nor everlastingly study to secure for his use the best of the bait, nor always fail to return borrowed tackle, nor prove to be blind, deaf and dumb when others are in tackle need, nor crowd into another's place, nor draw his flask in secrecy, nor light a cigar with no suggestion of another, nor do a score of other indefinable mean things that among true fishermen constitute him an unbearable nuisance, he will not only be tolerated but aided in every possible way. . . .

A true fisherman is conservative, provident, not given to envy, considerate of the rights of others, and careful of his good name. He fishes many a day and returns at night to his home, hungry, tired and disappointed; but he still has faith in his methods and is not tempted to try new and more deadly lures. On the contrary, he is willing in all circumstances to give the fish the chance for life which a liberal sporting disposition has determined to be their due. . . ."

Stempel, who as a matter of course rarely agrees with me, grunts.

We pull off the highway at Bethel and head for the river. At the river, we suit up and wade into water above the iron bridge. A cocoon of mist envelops us. Syl is right, the fish are biting. And true to form, he ultimately catches twice as many fish as I do. But how can I be jealous? We are not out here just to snare fish but to enjoy the air, landscape, the sounds of rushing water.

On the way back to Burlington, I read to him from a letter from Cleveland to his buddy, the actor Joe Jefferson:

"Did it ever occur to you what a fortunate thing it is that you and I jointly are able to appreciate and enjoy a regular out-and-out outing, undisturbed by the question of fish captured? How many of our excursions have been thus redeemed! It really seems to be a kind of low, sordid view to take of our excursions, to measure their success by the number of poor, slimy fish we are able to exhibit."

Stempel turns to me with the kind of expression he usually reserves for tax dodgers from New Jersey.

"Yeah, right!"

NOTES

INTRODUCTION

1. I would also have been tripping over two authors who produced a fine volume on the chief executives and golf. Shepherd Campbell and Peter Landau, *Presidential Lies* (New York: Macmillan), 1996.

CHAPTER ONE

1. *Diaries of George Washington,* Vol. 5, Donald Jackson and Dorothy Twohig, eds. (Charlottesville: University Press of Virginia), 1979, pp. 178-80.
2. *Diaries of George Washington,* Vol. 1, Donald Jackson, ed. (Charlottesville: University Press of Virginia), 1976, p. 46.
3. *Diaries of George Washington,* Donald Jackson, ed. (Charlottesville: University Press of Virginia), 1976, 1978, Vol. 2, p. 64, pp. 269-71, pp. 299-301; vol. 3, p. 124.
4. All in all, though, Washington wrote sparsely of his sport fishing. He never felt the need to describe the weather conditions or his tackle. In fact, the only artifact of fishing at Mount Vernon is a lacquered "fishing case for the pocket," a snuff box–size container of lines and hooks which sits in a display case among the wigs, pewter, and quill pens. Kenneth Reinard of Lititz, Pa., has turned his fascination with early fishing techniques into a public hobby. As "the Colonial Angler," the outdoor shop clerk offers demonstrations of the techniques he surmises colonial anglers such as Washington would have used. He makes lines out of braided horsehair, his hooks from sewing needles, his fly patterns from Dame Juliana Berners' treatise on fishing and ties his leaders direct to a ten-foot pole. (There were no reels in the eighteenth century.) He doubts that Washington made any of his own equipment. Reinard describes his interest and techniques in his book *The Colonial Angler's Manual of Flyfishing & Flytying* (Lancaster: Fox Chapel Publishing), 1995.
5. John Rhodehamel "Of Shad, Herring, &c." *Fairfax Chronicles,* Vol. VI, No. 1, published by the Office of Comprehensive Planning, Fairfax County, Virginia, February-April, 1982, p. 2. Used by permission of the author.

6. *Papers of George Washington,* Vol. 9, W. W. Abbot and Dorothy Twohig, eds. (Charlottesville: University Press of Virginia), 1994, p. 60.

7. *Diaries of George Washington,* Vol. 5, W. W. Abbot, ed. (Charlottesville: University Press of Virginia), 1988, pp. 214-15.

8. April 24, 1796. *Writings of George Washington,* Vol. 35, John C. Fitzpatrick, ed. (Washington: U.S. Government Printing Office), 1940, p. 25.

9. April 12, 1794. Ibid., Vol. 33, p. 326.

10. March 23, 1794. Ibid., Vol. 33, p. 302.

11. Ibid., Vol. 34, pp. 126, 145.

12. January 12, 1773. *Papers of George Washington,* Vol. 9, W. W. Abbot and Dorothy Twohig, eds. (Charlottesville: University Press of Virginia), 1994, p. 159.

13. *Writings of George Washington,* Vol. 22, John C. Fitzpatrick, ed. (Washington: U.S. Government Printing Office), 1937, pp. 7-8.

14. Ibid., pp. 35-36

15. Ibid., Vol. 34, p. 417.

16. Ibid., Vol. 29, p. 256.

CHAPTER TWO

1. Ruth Painter Randall, *Lincoln's Sons* (Boston: Little, Brown), 1955, p. 45.

2. Paul Schullery, "Theodore Roosevelt as an Angler," *The American Fly Fisher,* Summer 1982, pp. 20-26.

3. Theodore Roosevelt, *Diaries of Boyhood and Youth* (New York: Charles Scribner's Sons), 1928, pp. 245-48.

4. Herbert Hoover, *Fishing for Fun* (West Branch: Hoover Presidential Library), 1964, pp. 35-38.

5. Hoover, *Fishing for Fun,* pp. 82-83.

6. Ed Mason, "Ike's First Fishing Hole," *Rod and Gun,* March 1955, pp. 5, 42.

7. This description of Bush's early fishing is drawn from an interview he did with *Fly Rod & Reel* magazine in April 1989 and recollections he gave to his friend and guide, Maine angler Bob Boilard, who shared them with me (August 18, 1995).

8. Jimmy Carter, *An Outdoor Journal* (Fayetteville: University of Arkansas Press), 1994, pp. 25-27.

9. Carter, *An Outdoor Journal,* pp. 33-34.

CHAPTER THREE

1. The first draft of this chapter strained to be witty. I conceived two new campaign devices: The A.A., or Advance Angler, would scout out opportunities for a candidate to appeal to the fishing bloc of voters. The other was a P.P.P.P., or Presidential Piscatorial Potency Poll, which would measure the electoral appeal of a candidate catching a bream, trout, catfish, etc. The more primary sources I found, the less humorous I became, and I gave these gimmicks an honorable discharge.

2. The Rogers quote is from his *How We Elect Our Presidents,* Hoover's from *Fishing for Fun,* and Bush's from a personal interview.

3. Herbert Hoover, *Fishing for Fun,* ed. William Nichols (West Branch: Herbert Hoover Presidential Library), 1963, pp. 69-70.

4. Gil Troy, *See How They Ran* (Cambridge: Harvard University Press), 1996.

5. James Flexner, *Washington: The Independent Man* (Boston: Little, Brown), 1974, p. 229.

6. *Diaries of George Washington,* Vol. 5, Donald Jackson and Dorothy Twohig, eds. (Charlottesville: University Press of Virginia), 1979, pp. 488-90.

7. Brewster, *Rambles about Portsmouth,* Ser. I (Portsmouth), 1873, p. 266.

8. A detailed account of Arthur's trip appears in *Montana, the Magazine of Western History,* Summer 1969, Vol. XIX, No. 3, pp. 18-29, by Thomas Reeves, who subsequently wrote an excellent biography of Arthur, *Gentleman Boss* (New York: A. A. Knopf), 1975.

9. G. G. Vest, "Notes of the Yellowstone Trip," *Forest and Stream,* Vol. XXI, November 8, 1883, p. 282.

10. Eugene Field, *Poems of Eugene Field* (New York: Scribners), 1912, pp. 445-46.

11. Allan Nevins, *Grover Cleveland: A Study in Courage* (New York: Dodd, Mead), 1932, p. 305.

12. I rely here on Nevins plus Paul Lancaster's *Gentleman of the Press, The Life and Times of Julian Ralph* (Syracuse: Syracuse Univ. Press), 1992, pp. 118-22. The letter to the *Evening Post* is from the Cleveland Papers, June 21, 1886, and is reprinted in Nevins, p. 307.

13. Nevins, Grover Cleveland, pp. 520-21.

14. Grover Cleveland, *Fishing and Shooting Sketches* (New York: The Outing Publishing Company), 1906, pp. 4-5.

15. Troy, *See How They Ran,* p. 95.

16. Edward Lindop and Joe Jares, *White House Sportsmen* (Boston: Houghton Mifflin), 1964, p. 78.

17. Susan Kismaric, *American Politicians: Photographs from 1843 to 1993* (New York: Museum of Modern Art), 1994, pp. 17–18.

18. *Letters of Theodore Roosevelt,* Vol. 6 (Cambridge: Harvard University Press), 1952, pp. 1209–10.

19. See Troy, *See How They Ran,* ch. 7, "Reluctant Runners."

20. Paul Schullery, "Theodore Roosevelt as an Angler," *The American Fly Fisher,* Summer 1982, p. 20.

21. The following section is drawn from the *New York Times* of November 9–11, 1920.

22. *New York Times,* November 11, 1920.

23. *New York Times,* July 5, 1928.

24. *New York Herald Tribune,* July 31, 1928.

25. Will Rogers, *How We Elect Our Presidents,* selected and edited by Donald Day (Boston: Little, Brown), 1952, p. 130. This book was one of those wonderfully serendipitous finds of research. I was looking through the U.S. history section of a rural Vermont used book store and happened upon both this and Merriman Smith's volume on Eisenhower.

26. Ibid., p. 134.

27. Hugh Gregory Gallagher, *FDR's Splendid Deception* (New York: Dodd, Mead), 1985, pp. 111–12. This quote is from James Roosevelt, *My Parents: A Differing View* (Chicago: Playboy Press), 1976, p. 84.

28. Dorothy Thompson, "On the Record" column, "Fishing in Politics," *New York Herald Tribune,* April 9, 1936. Here is another example of stumbling into a good source. I came across this while reading Peter Kurth's engaging biography of Thompson.

29. Much later, Hoover, Jimmy Carter, and George Bush became enthusiastic bonefishers.

30. Dixon Wechter, *The Hero in America* (New York: Charles Scribner), 1941, p. 485. Wechter was obviously comparing Franklin D. Roosevelt to his two predecessors, Hoover and Coolidge, who never seemed to be out of coat and tie. Thus far had public presidential angling advanced that for this observer in 1941, it would be a given that a candidate/president would fish.

31. An interesting question is whether "political" fishing may be easier for nonangling politicians because they don't become frustrated at being kept from the real thing.

32. Brent Frazee, *Kansas City Star.*

33. Richard Nixon, *In the Arena* (New York: Simon & Schuster), 1990, pp. 163-64.

34. Reprinted courtesy of *Sports Illustrated,* April 25, 1955. Copyright 1955, Time Inc. "V.P.'s Fish Story," by James Shepley. All rights reserved.

35. Merriman Smith, *Meet Mister Eisenhower* (New York: Harper & Row), 1955, pp. 133-50.

36. Knowlton Nash, *Kennedy & Diefenbaker* (Toronto: McClelland & Stewart), 1991, pp. 96-97.

37. Jimmy Carter, *An Outdoor Journal* (Fayetteville: University of Arkansas Press), 1994, p. 79.

38. Bob Boilard, interview by author, August 1994.

39. George Bush, interview by author, August 1995.

40. Carolyn Meub, interview by author, November 1995.

41. *Portland (Maine) Press,* September 4, 1989.

42. All the Bush quotes are from my interview with him at Kennebunkport in August 1995. I asked him if he felt the press was ever "mean" about his fishing:

> No, except for the kidding about not catching fish. The press wasn't mean. The rabbit story got mean because it tied in with a certain impression of Jimmy Carter—"Yeah, attacked by a rabbit!"

CHAPTER FOUR

1. The Hoover quotes are from his *Fishing for Fun,* the FDR quote is from a press conference in 1937, the Jimmy Carter quote is from his book *An Outdoor Journal,* and the Bush quote is from a personal interview with the author.

2. From an interview by the author with Boilard in August 1995.

3. Herbert Hoover, *Fishing for Fun* (West Branch: Hoover Presidential Library), 1963, p. 76.

4. Interview by author, August 1995.

5. Arthur was not the first president to vacation in this community. Martin Van Buren visited the area. And Ulysses S. Grant was a guest of the Pullman family in 1872 after his nomination for a second term.

6. "President Grant Falls in River," *Thousand Islands Sun,* Alexandria Bay, N.Y., May 27, 1976, p. 4.

7. I am indebted to Paul Lancaster and his biography of Julian Ralph, *Gentleman of the Press* (Syracuse: Syracuse Univ. Press), 1992, for introducing me to that intrepid journalist and his detailed dispatches about Arthur's sojourn in Alexandria Bay. The quotes from those dispatches that follow are all from the *New York Sun,* September 28 to October 8, 1882.

8. *New York World,* quoted in Allan Nevins, *Grover Cleveland: A Study in Courage* (New York: Dodd, Mead), 1932, pp. 244-45.

9. Information on Cleveland's fishing escapes comes from Nevins's Pulitzer Prize-winning biography, *Grover Cleveland.*

10. Edward Lindop and Joe Jares, *White House Sportsmen* (Boston: Houghton Mifflin), 1964, p. 75.

11. Nevins, *Grover Cleveland,* pp. 741-42.

12. Theodore Roosevelt, *Through the Brazilian Wilderness* (New York: Charles Scribner's Sons), 1920, p. 384.

13. Paul Schullery, "Theodore Roosevelt as an Angler," *The American Fly Fisher,* Summer 1982, pp. 25-26. I am indebted to both Paul Schullery and Roosevelt's great-grandson Tweed for alerting me to this adventure. Tweed Roosevelt contends that it was TR who "popularized" the piranha and made it a widespread image of voraciousness.

14. *New York Times,* June 22, 1927, p. 17.

15. Edmund Starling, as told to Thomas Sugrue, *Starling of the White House* (New York: Simon & Schuster), 1946, pp. 252-53.

16. This paragraph is based upon a letter from amateur historian Russ Soli of Brookfield, Wisconsin, to Ms. Cindy Bittinger, the executive director of the Calvin Coolidge Memorial Foundation, October 31, 1990.

17. John Hiram McKee, *Coolidge Wit and Wisdom* (New York: Frederick A. Stokes), 1933, p. 21.

18. Ruth Dennis, *The Homes of the Hoovers* (West Branch: Herbert Hoover Presidential Library Association), 1986, pp. 47-50.

19. Richard N. Smith, *An Uncommon Man* (New York: Simon & Schuster), 1983, pp. 34-35.

20. Starling, *Starling of the White House,* pp. 283-84.

21. Letter from Adams to Congressman Henry T. Rainey, August 1, 1932.

22. Hoover, *Fishing for Fun,* p. 18.

23. "After Hoover left office, he deeded the property to the Virginia Department of Conservation and Development. For ten years the camp was used as a Boy Scout retreat, and in 1958 it was transferred to the National Park Service. The Rapidan retreat is now a part of the

Shenandoah National Park and 'Camp Hoover' may be visited during the summer months. Three of the original buildings remain and the Park Service plans to restore the camp to its 1929-33 appearance." Dana Lemaster, "Hoover Was Here," *Washington Post,* July 16, 1997, p. D9.

24. Letter to George Mathew Adams, July 29, 1944, Darling Papers, University of Iowa Libraries, Iowa City, Iowa. Cited in David Lendt, *Ding: The Life of Jay Norwood Darling* (Ames: Iowa State Univ. Press), 1979, p. 50. According to a research archivist at the Hoover Presidential Library, the drawing refers to a fishing outing that Hoover took with Eisenhower in 1954 and how intrusive the press were. From this trip probably came the famous observation that presidents had now lost fishing as one of their only two times of solitude. The "Dinosaur Monument Atrocity" was a U.S. Corps of Engineers plan to construct the Echo Park Dam on the upper Colorado River in Utah. Darling was appalled at this reversal of what he considered sound national conservation policy. In addition to his drawing pen, Darling used his typewriter and voice to lobby for this and a range of conservation issues.

25. James Roosevelt, *Affectionately, F.D.R.* (New York: Harcourt, Brace), 1962, pp. 162-67.

26. Another informal name given the room by the staff was the Morgue because guests often had to "cool off" there waiting for the President to receive them. Cited in William Hassett, *Off the Record with F.D.R.* (New Brunswick: Rutgers Univ. Press), 1958, p. 312.

27. William Rigdon, *White House Sailor* (Garden City: Doubleday), 1962, pp. 44, 60, 97-99. After his polio, Roosevelt did very little freshwater fishing except at Warm Springs and Shangri-La. Two exceptions were a 1943 vacation to the South Carolina estate of financier Bernard Baruch and a short excursion with Churchill when the two met in Quebec, Canada, that same year.

28. Rigdon, *White House Sailor,* pp. 60-62.

29. Harold Ickes, *The Secret Diaries of Harold L. Ickes,* Vol. 1 (New York: Simon & Schuster), 1953, pp. 449-50.

30. FDR's 366th Press Conference, May 13, 1937. Held on the President's train en route from Galveston, Texas, to Washington, D.C. Courtesy F.D.R. Library.

31. Rigdon, *White House Sailor,* pp. 213-19.

32. Shepherd Campbell and Peter Landau, *Presidential Lies* (New York: Macmillan), 1996, p. 108.

33. Press conference, October 15, 1958.

34. Alfred M. Lansing, "Ike's Fishing Secrets," *Collier's* magazine, April 15, 1955, pp. 31–33.

35. Lindop and Jares, *White House Sportsmen,* p. 80.

Former U.S. Senator Mark Hatfield (R–Oregon) worked with and under Hoover while a graduate student at Stanford. Hoover treated him as almost a surrogate son. Although Hatfield was not much of a fisherman, he knew well Hoover's passion for the sport and heard many of the ex-president's observations.

Truman and Roosevelt may have escaped into the sea in part because they wanted to get out of the range of the press. In Mr. Hoover's day, there was much more privacy, seclusion and more opportunity to escape. He was not gregarious and fishing was one of those marvelous compensations. Today, you can't even get into the wilderness areas without the tenacious press right there. Can you imagine a President today getting off by himself, as Hoover did on the Rogue River, or as Cleveland did in the Adirondacks?

Today, Hoover's comment to Eisenhower is more true than ever—Presidents can't even fish in seclusion. Prayer is the only activity left and I'm sure that if they could, the media would take pictures of this or listen in to what the Presidents might say to the Lord.

36. Richard Nixon, *In the Arena* (New York: Simon & Schuster), 1990, p. 160.

37. Jimmy Carter, *An Outdoor Journal* (Fayetteville: University of Arkansas Press), 1994, p. 73.

38. Interview with author, July 1995.

39. Carter, *An Outdoor Journal,* pp. 120–22.

40. Carter, *An Outdoor Journal,* p. 122.

41. Howell Raines, "In Fly Fishing, Carter's Record Can't Be Assailed," *New York Times,* May 4, 1991.

42. Remarks reprinted in *The American Fly Fisher,* Fall 1981, Vol. 8, No. 4, p. 7.

43. Interview with author, August 1995.

44. Ibid.

CHAPTER FIVE

1. Permissions for use of the cartoons are listed chronologically at the back of the book.
2. Quoted in *Time* magazine, Stefan Kanfer, "Editorial Cartoons: Capturing the Essence," February 3, 1975, p. 63.
3. According to Darling's biographer David Lendt, this quote was part of an unpublished speech that the cartoonist gave to a gathering of insurance company executives in New York City in 1928.
4. Drawn from a memo by FDR about the secret rendezvous, reprinted in James Roosevelt, *Affectionately, F.D.R.* (New York: Harcourt, Brace), 1959, pp. 334–38. Son Elliott Roosevelt, in his short memoir of being a wartime aide to his father, wrote that FDR was tickled that his fishing subterfuge had fooled the press. "They think I'm fishing somewhere off the Bay of Fundy." The next day he actually did some bottom fishing in Argentia harbor and, according to Elliott, caught a "What-Is-It," unidentifiable by anyone on board. FDR suggested that it be sent to the Smithsonian Institution for identification. Elliott Roosevelt, *As He Saw It* (New York: Duell, Sloan and Pearce), 1946, pp. 19–20.
5. Stephen Hess and Milton Kaplan, *The Ungentlemanly Art* (New York: Macmillan), 1975.
6. Linda Mullins, *The Teddy Bear Men: Theodore Roosevelt and Clifford Berryman* (Cumberland: Hobby House), 1987, p. 143.
7. This collection, developed by Roosevelt's early law partner, was one of those wonderful discoveries researchers occasionally happen upon. When I was beginning my work on this book, a research assistant at the FDR Library suggested in passing that I might find a few items in those several bound volumes of over twelve thousand cartoons in tearsheet form that were assembled chronologically. Once I found the dates of Roosevelt's fishing vacations, I invariably found several fishing-based cartoons.
8. Jay N. Darling, *As Ding Saw Hoover,* ed. John Henry (Ames: Iowa State College Press), 1954.
9. Other Seibel fishing cartoons are sprinkled throughout this book.
10. Quoted in Charles McDowell Jr., "Fred O. Seibel," *Richmond Times-Dispatch,* June 24, 1956.

CHAPTER SIX

1. Grover Cleveland, *Fishing and Shooting Sketches* (New York: The Outing Publishing Co.), 1906, p. 106.
2. Quoted in Chas. Z. Southard, *The Evolution of Trout and Trout Fishing in America* (New York: E. P. Dutton), 1928.
3. Interview with author, August 1995.
4. Cleveland, *Fishing and Shooting Sketches,* p. 28.
5. The poet Eugene Field, who had celebrated Chester A. Arthur's trip to Yellowstone Park and who would commemorate Cleveland's White House wedding to Frances Folsom, also captured the "fish that got away." In a contemporary poem, one stanza reads:

   > And really, fish look bigger than they are before they're caught—
   > When the pole is bent into a bow and the slender line is taut,
   > When a fellow feels his heart rise up like a doughnut in his throat
   > And he lunges in a frenzy up and down a leaky boat!
   > Oh, you who've been a-fishing will indorse me when I say
   > That it always is the biggest fish you catch that gets away!

   Eugene Field, *The Poems of Eugene Field* (New York: Charles Scribner's Sons), 1911.
6. Cleveland, *Fishing and Shooting Sketches,* pp. 34–35.
7. Cleveland, *Fishing and Shooting Sketches,* pp. 105-7.
8. Charles Goodspeed, *Angling in America* (Boston: Houghton Mifflin), 1939, p. 314.
9. *New York Times,* June 17, 1927, p. 12.
10. Letter to the author.
11. Herbert Hoover, *Fishing for Fun* (West Branch: Hoover Presidential Library), 1963, p. 31.
12. Hoover, *Fishing for Fun,* p. 21.
13. James Roosevelt, *Affectionately, F.D.R.* (New York: Harcourt, Brace), 1959, op. cit. p. 281.
14. Jimmy Carter, *An Outdoor Journal,* (Fayetteville: University of Arkansas Press), 1994, p. 9.
15. Larry Sabato, *Feeding Frenzy* (New York: Free Press), 1991, pp. 74–75.

16. Brooks Jackson, interview with author, August 1995. The original dispatch is printed below.

> WASHINGTON, Aug. 29 [1979] A "killer rabbit" penetrated Secret Service security and attacked President Carter on a recent trip to Plains, Ga., according to White House staff members who said that the President beat back the animal with a canoe paddle.
>
> The rabbit, which the President later guessed was fleeing in panic from some predator, reportedly swam toward the canoe from which Mr. Carter was fishing in a pond. It was said to have been hissing menacingly, its teeth flashing and its nostrils flared, and making straight for the President.
>
> Mr. Carter was not injured, and reports were unclear about what became of the rabbit. But a White House staff photographer made a picture of the attack and the President's successful self-defense. This was fortunate because some of the President's closest staff members reportedly refused to believe the story when Mr. Carter told them about the attack later.
>
> "Everybody knows rabbits don't swim," one staff member said.
>
> Mr. Carter, said to be stung by this skepticism in his inner circle, ordered a print of the photograph. But this was not good enough.
>
> "You could see him in the canoe with his paddle raised, and you could see something in the water," said the doubter. "But you couldn't tell what it was. It could have been anything."
>
> So Mr. Carter ordered an enlargement. "It's the rabbit, all right," the staff member said after seeing the blown-up photo.
>
> Another staff member who saw the picture agreed. "It was a killer rabbit," this staff member said. "The President was swinging for his life."
>
> No news photographers were allowed within camera range of Mr. Carter on the fishing trip, which was made on April 20. And the White House declined to make public any photographs of the encounter with the rabbit. "There are just certain stories about the President that must forever remain shrouded in mystery," Rex Granum, the deputy White House press secretary, said today.

17. Edward Zern, *Hunting and Fishing From "A" to Zern* (New York: Lyons & Burford), 1985, pp. 114–15.

CHAPTER SEVEN

1. Note, FDR to H. M. McIntyre, January 13, 1937, President's Personal File 267. Franklin D. Roosevelt Library.
2. Jimmy Carter to James Baker, January 14, 1988.
3. James Baker to Jimmy Carter, February 17, 1988.
4. Letter from Harvey B. Fox, director, Office of Regulations and Rulings, U.S. Customs Service, to Steven Newman of Newman, Wilson & Co. Inc., Portland, Oregon, March 4, 1988. Newman was one of the outfitters who had protested against the fly packaging regulations. A copy of the letter is in the files of the Jimmy Carter Library.
5. Baker's letter to Carter is dated March 21, 1988. Carter's reply was scribbled on Baker's letter and sent back to the secretary on March 24, 1988.
6. *Harper's Weekly,* Aug. 25, 1906, p. 126.
7. G. C. to Richard Gilder, July 23, 1898. *Letters of Grover Cleveland,* ed. Allan Nevins (Boston: Houghton Mifflin), 1933, p. 486.
8. *Forest & Stream,* February 1896.
9. For the years 1982–85, the club sent President Ronald Reagan the first salmon.
10. Tom Hennessey, "The Penobscot's Presidential Salmon," *Bangor Daily News,* May 2–3, 1987.
11. *Bangor Daily News,* April 7, 1916.
12. Herbert Hoover, *Fishing for Fun* (West Branch: Hoover Presidential Library), 1963, pp. 80–81.
    Edmund Starling, the Secret Service chief, tells the story, with himself at the center of the action:

> [The Congressman had] sent it to the White House by messenger, intending to come by later to be photographed with the fish and the President. Meanwhile efficiency, working at a mad clip, shuttled the fish to the White House kitchen, where its head was removed and it was set aside to be prepared for cooking. All was chaos. The Congressman wondered what he would say to the folks back home. I felt so sorry for him that I decided to make an attempt at saving the situation. I got a needle and thread and sewed the head back on the fish's body. The picture

was taken and Maine did not go Democratic for three years. Edmund Starling, *Starling of the White House* (New York: Simon & Schuster), 1946, pp. 284–85.

13. To learn what happened to the prisoner took six months of correspondence with the Wyoming Historical Society, the state archives, and the department of corrections. The final result meant far more to the writer than to the readers.

14. Dwight Eisenhower letter to Joseph D. Bates Jr., February 10, 1956, shared with author by Pamela Bates Richards.

15. Related to author by Farrow Allen.

16. Letter to author from Dean Minton.

17. *New York Sun,* September 29, 1882.

18. Grover Cleveland, *Fishing and Shooting Sketches,* (New York: The Outing Publishing Company), 1906, p. 4.

19. Curran's letter is dated August 19, 1932, and Hoover's reply is August 23, 1932. It's worth noting that on Hoover's first fishing trip after his November defeat, he caught three sailfish in Florida.

20. Baas's column appeared in *Wisconsin State Journal* in mid-June 1955. Eisenhower aide Bryce Harlow thanked Reuss for sending the column without saying whether Ike had ever read it.

21. Telegram, August 2, 1957.

22. Letter of James Hagerty to Edward Barrows, vice president, League of Salt Water Anglers, Providence, Rhode Island, August 8, 1957.

23. On a visit to Humphrey shortly before his death, I asked if he would "reconstruct" his letter to Carter. Without hesitation, he wrote down these words.

24. William Nichols, ed., *On Growing Up* (New York: William Morrow), 1962, p. 77.

CHAPTER EIGHT

1. Herbert Hoover, *Fishing for Fun,* (West Branch: Hoover Presidential Library), 1963, pp. 30–31.

The outdoor writer Ed Zern, with gentle gibes, quotes a nineteenth century British book on pike fishing, which ascribes angelic qualities to the angler: "For we may observe that the fisherman is a kindly man, not given to lustful excess or vile thought, but marked by gentility of word and deed. . . ." Malarky, says Zern. Quoted in *Ed Zern, Hunting and Fishing from "A" to Zern* (New York: Lyons & Burford), 1985, p. 64.

2. Finley Peter Dunne in "Swearing," *Observations by Mr. Dooley* (New York: R. H. Russell), 1902.

3. George Dawson, *The Pleasures of Angling* (New York: Sheldon & Co.), 1876, pp. 130-31.

4. Edmund Starling, as told to Thomas Sugrue, *Starling of the White House* (New York: Simon & Schuster), 1946, p. 267.

5. "Remarks of the President from the U.S.S. *Potomac* in the harbor of Ft. Lauderdale, Florida, March 29, 1941." Courtesy of FDR Library, Hyde Park, N.Y. After these lighthearted remarks, Roosevelt proceeded to a somber assessment of the world situation and the need for national unity in the face of the twin perils of Nazism and Japanese imperialism.

6. John Gunther, *Roosevelt in Retrospect* (New York: Harper & Brothers), 1950, p. 83.

7. Alfred M. Lansing, "Ike's Fishing Secrets," *Collier's* magazine, April 15, 1955, p. 33.

8. Jimmy Carter, *An Outdoor Journal,* (Fayetteville: University of Arkansas Press), 1994, pp. 77-79.

9. Grover Cleveland, *Fishing and Shooting Sketches,* (New York: The Outing Publishing Company), 1906, pp. 40-45.

CHAPTER NINE

1. Grover Cleveland, *Fishing and Shooting Sketches,* (New York: The Outing Publishing Company), 1906, p. 98.

2. Herbert Hoover, *Fishing for Fun,* (West Branch: Hoover Presidential Library), 1963, p. 32.

3. Jimmy Carter, *An Outdoor Journal,* (Fayetteville: University of Arkansas Press), 1994, p. 11.

4. Irwin H. Hoover, *Forty-two Years in the White House* (Boston: Houghton Mifflin), 1934, p. 249.

5. *Letters of Grover Cleveland,* ed. Allan Nevins (Boston: Houghton Mifflin), 1933, pp. 401-2; letter dated July 10, 1895.

6. *Letters of Grover Cleveland,* p. 516; letter dated June 16, 1899.

7. John J. O'Leary Jr., *Talks with T.R.* (Boston: Houghton Mifflin), 1920, pp. 166-68.

8. Theodore Roosevelt, "Harpooning Devilfish," *Scribner's* magazine, Vol. LXII, No. 3, p. 294.

9. O'Leary, *Talks with T.R.,* pp. 168-72.

10. Edmund Starling, *Starling of the White House,* (New York: Simon & Schuster), 1946, pp. 241-42.
The following description shows the former president back in Vermont fishing on his own terms, without the benefit of Starling's self-promoting tutelage.

During the fishing season the customary procedure was about as follows: Mr. Coolidge would say to John, the chauffeur and myself, "If you will dig some of the old worms we will go catch the fish." Whereupon John and I would proceed to Aurora Pierce's (who by the way is a great character and has been the Coolidge housekeeper at Plymouth for over thirty years) . . . garden patch and fill an old tin can full of worms. Then in the Lincoln sedan [that] Mr. Coolidge brought back from Washington we would drive about a half a mile to the brook. Mr. Coolidge always fished in a business suit complete with white shirt and high collar, the only deviation from his customary dress being that he would pull on a pair of hip boots, which he usually wore turned down at the knee. Upon arrival at the brook we would put the rod together, and instruct the chauffeur to return home. For no reason that I could ever figure out, I always was encumbered with an aluminum rod case with an extra tip. I don't believe [Coolidge] ever broke a rod tip in his life, certainly never on those fish up there, and it used to make me laugh to think of the picture it would have made. Then I had the creel to carry, in which were the can of worms and a six inch portion of an old carpenter's rule. Mr. Coolidge was very particular about the length and I am sure never kept one a hair under six inches. Instead of his carrying the worms where they would be handy, I had them and usually had to bait his hook for him and was always on the opposite side of the brook. He would often give them the butt, and I really got so that I could almost tell the length of the fish as I saw it fly through the air. They would often fly off the hook, and then [I] had to search through the bog, marsh or long grass until [I] found it and returned it to the brook. Once in a while it was impossible to find "Mr. Trout," and on these occasions I used to fool the chief a bit by making a little splash in the brook when he was not looking. Mr. Coolidge was not one of those fisher-

men who wanted to make a large catch but was seemingly satisfied with a few.

There were a couple of ponds up there that he used to fish
on now and then, and there he always used a fly when I rowed
the boat. In my opinion he was only a very ordinary fly caster
as he was inclined to be a bit slow on the strike on the rise.
Every summer he used to go with Attorney General Sargent, of
Ludlow, to two or three different small clubs in the state. . . .

Quoted in Charles Goodspeed, *Angling in America* (Boston: Houghton
Mifflin), 1939, pp. 330-31.

11. The Bowers and Albury quotes come from interviews conducted by
    Hoover Library director Raymond Henle at Key West, Florida, April
    14, 1967.
12. Log of the inspection cruise and fishing expedition of President
    Franklin D. Roosevelt on board the USS *Houston,* July 16-August 9,
    1938, courtesy the FDR Library, Hyde Park, New York. Excerpts
    from the ship's log captured the jocular tone of good friends who hap-
    pen to fish together:

    Wednesday 20 July
    The poor fishing luck of the previous day whetted the pisca-
    torial anticipations of the President and his party, all of whom
    eagerly embarked in the fishing boats as soon as they were
    hoisted out. The reward was nearly three hours of excellent
    fishing, the waters in and near Braithwaite Bay abounding in
    fish of all species, particularly groupers of which a large number
    were caught. The honor for hauling in the largest fish of the
    morning went to the President, by virtue of a Jack [that] tipped
    the scales at thirty-eight pounds. This streamlined finny "Crit-
    ter" put up quite a battle before he was landed, affording the
    President the best of sport. Honors for the largest catch went to
    the boat occupied by "Doc" McIntire and Steve Early [press
    secretary] with a total of 48—a sizeable catch for the less than
    three hours of sport. Much to his discomfort, "Pa" Watson did
    not participate in either of the day's fishing prizes. Much
    chaffing at the dinner table ensued over Pa's failure to "bring
    home the bacon" by his so-called "Commercialized"
    methods. . . .

Thursday 21 July

Despite a somewhat choppy sea and moderate swell, the Presidential party took to the fishing boats shortly after luncheon for a resumption of fishing activities after a twenty-four hour respite. Hardly had the President's boat shoved off from the *Houston* before he hooked and landed a sixty-pound shark—a forerunner of the type [that] played havoc with fishing tackle and spoiled, after a fashion, the day's sport. For, hardly had one hooked a Grouper, Jack, or Yellow Tail before it was snatched bodily by a voracious Shark. The waters in this area are literally alive with them as with other species as well. Steve Early had a monumental struggle with a 175-pound Shark for an hour and forty minutes, finally passing the combat to another member of the party when cramped leg muscles cried for relief.

Anent Sharks, much argument ensued at the dinner table this night as to whether or not a shark was, in reality, a fish and should or should not count in the day's catch as to size and quantity. Pa [Watson] contended that the "revolting Shark" was not *edible* (none contested this statement!) and therefore should not be counted. Arguments pro and con were settled when the President announced his decision that now and henceforth Sharks would be counted as part of the day's catch.

13. The Barney Farley quotes are taken from an undated typed manuscript, "President Roosevelt as I Knew Him, by Barney Farley—His Fishing Guide," courtesy the FDR Library.
14. Interview with author, February 1996.
15. *New York Times,* March 16, 1947.
16. *New York Times,* March 6-19, 1949.
17. *New York Times,* March 8, 1949.
18. Stephen Ambrose, "The General Goes Fishing," *Wisconsin Trails,* July–August 1982, pp. 40-42.
19. Milford K. Smith, "Stray Shots and Short Casts," *Rutland (Vt.) Herald,* July 4, 1955.
20. Harold Blaisdell, *The Philosophical Fisherman* (New York: Nick Lyons Books), 1969, p. 110.
21. Jimmy Carter, *An Outdoor Journal* (Fayetteville: University of Arkansas Press), 1994, p. 121.

22. William S. McFeeley, *Grant* (New York: W. W. Norton), 1981, p. 23.
23. *New York Daily Graphic,* May 26, 1878.
24. Letter to Dr. Curtis W. Garrison, director of the Hayes Memorial, Fremont, Ohio, from Mrs. Frances Hayes (President Hayes's only daughter), July 7, 1941.
25. *New York Times,* November 9 and 11, 1920.
26. *New York Times,* June 21, 1927, p. 17.
27. Interview with author.
28. Carter, *An Outdoor Journal,* pp. 101-2.
29. Carter, *An Outdoor Journal,* p. 74.
30. Interview with author, May 1995.
31. Interview with author, June 1995.
32. Interview with author, July 1995.
33. Don Daughenbaugh, letter to author, September 1997.
34. Material from Boilard was collected over several years between 1994 and 1997, through both face-to-face and telephone interviews. Getting to know him and to hear more about his work as an environmental gadfly was one of the ancillary delights of researching the presidents.
35. Interview with author, August 1995.

CHAPTER TEN

1. Paul Schullery, *American Fly Fishing: A History* (New York, Lyons & Burford), 1987, pp. 247–48.
2. Herbert Hoover, *Fishing for Fun* (West Branch: Herbert Hoover Presidential Library), 1963, pp. 33-34.
3. *Burlington Free Press,* June 18, 1927, from AP dispatch of June 17, 1927.
4. Edmund Starling, as told to Thomas Sugrue, *Starling of the White House* (New York: Simon & Schuster), 1946, p. 250.
5. Dorothy Weyandt, *I Was a Guide for Three U.S. Presidents,* privately published, 1976, pp. 246-47.
6. Frederic Van de Water, *In Defense of Worms and Other Angling Heresies* (New York: Duell, Sloan, and Pearce), 1949, pp. 71-72. It was a pity that Coolidge never got a chance to read this.
7. Herbert Hoover Presidential Library.
8. Edward Lindop and Joseph Jares, *White House Sportsmen* (Boston: Houghton Mifflin), 1964, p. 74.
9. *Pictorial Biography of Harry S. Truman* (New York: Grosset & Dunlop), 1975, p. 99.

10. Jimmy Carter, *An Outdoor Journal* (Fayetteville: University of Arkansas Press), 1994, pp. 67–68, 72–73.

11. Don Zahner, *Anglish Spoken Here* (Lexington: Stephen Greene Press), 1986, p. 142.

12. Howell Raines, "In Fly Fishing, Carter's Record Can't Be Assailed," *New York Times,* May 4, 1991.

13. Jim Merritt, "10th Angling President George Bush," *Fly Rod & Reel,* April 1989, pp. 26–27.

14. George Plimpton, *Sports Illustrated,* December 28, 1989, p. 147.

15. George Bush, "The Thrill of Northern Fishing," *Deh Cho Drum,* Ft. Simpson, Northwest Territories, September 4, 1997.

16. Grover Cleveland, *Fishing and Shooting Sketches,* (New York: The Outing Publishing Company), 1906, p. 118.

17. Cleveland, *Fishing and Shooting Sketches,* p. 123.

18. Cleveland, *Fishing and Shooting Sketches,* p. 116.

BIBLIOGRAPHY

Ambrose, Stephen E. "The General Goes Fishing." *Wisconsin Trails,* 1982.

Blaisdell, Harold F. *The Philosophical Fisherman.* Boston: Houghton Mifflin Company, 1969.

Blaisdell, Thomas C. Jr., and Peter Selz. Seminar, *The American Presidency in Political Cartoons: 1776–1976.* Berkeley: University Art Museum, 1976.

Boller, Paul F. Jr. *Presidential Anecdotes.* New York: Penguin Books, 1981.

Brasco, Katherine. *The Political Cartoons of Clifford K. Berryman.* Center for Legislative Archives. Washington: National Archives and Records Administration, 1995.

Brewster. *Rambles about Portsmouth,* Ser. I. Portsmouth,1873.

Bush, George. "The Thrill of Northern Fishing." *Deh Cho Drum,* September 4, 1997.

Campbell, Shepherd, and Peter Landau. *Presidential Lies.* New York: Macmillan, 1996.

Carter, Jimmy. *An Outdoor Journal.* Fayetteville, Ark.: University of Arkansas Press, 1994.

Cleveland, Grover. *Fishing and Shooting Sketches.* New York: The Outing Publishing Company, 1906.

Darling, J. N., and John M. Henry. *As Ding Saw Hoover.* Ames, Iowa: Iowa State College Press, 1954.

Dawson, George *The Pleasures of Angling.* New York: Sheldon & Co., 1876.

Dennis, Ruth. *The Homes of the Hoovers.* West Branch, Iowa: Herbert Hoover Presidential Library Association, 1986.

Dunne, Finley Peter. *Observations by Mr. Dooley.* New York: R. H. Russell, 1902.

Durant, John. *Sports of the Presidents.* New York: Hastings House, 1964.

Farley, Barney. "President Roosevelt as I Knew Him, by Barney Farley— His Fishing Guide." Typescript courtesy the Franklin D. Roosevelt Library, n.d.

Field, Eugene. *Poems of Eugene Field.* New York: Charles Scribner's Sons, 1912.

Flexner, James. *Washington: The Independent Man.* Boston: Little, Brown, 1974.

Gallagher, Hugh Gregory. *FDR's Splendid Deception.* New York: Dodd, Mead, 1985.

Goodspeed, Charles. *Angling in America.* Boston: Houghton Mifflin, 1939.

Gunther, John. *Roosevelt in Retrospect.* New York: Harper & Brothers, 1950.

Hassett, William. *Off the Record with F.D.R.* New Brunswick, N.J.: Rutgers University Press, 1958.

Hess, Stephen, and Milton Kaplan. *The Ungentlemanly Art: A History of American Political Cartoons.* New York: Macmillan, 1975.

Hoover, Herbert. *Fishing for Fun and to Wash Your Soul.* West Branch, Iowa: Herbert Hoover Presidential Library, 1963.

Hoover, Irwin. *Forty-two Years in the White House.* Boston: Houghton Mifflin, 1934.

Ickes, Harold. *The Secret Diaries of Harold L. Ickes,* Vol. 1. New York: Simon & Schuster, 1953.

Kanfer, Stefan. "Editorial Cartoons: Capturing the Essence." *Time,* Februrary 3, 1975.

Kismaric, Susan. *American Politicians: Photographs from 1843 to 1993.* New York: Museum of Modern Art, 1994.

Lancaster, Paul. *Gentleman of the Press: The Life and Times of an Early Reporter, Julian Ralph of the Sun.* Syracuse, N.Y.: Syracuse University Press, 1992.

Lansing, Alfred M. "Ike's Fishing Secrets." *Collier's,* April 15, 1955.

Lendt, David. *Ding: The Life of Jay Norwood Darling.* Ames, Iowa: Iowa State University Press, 1979.

Lindop, Edmund, and Joseph Jares. *White House Sportsmen.* Boston: Houghton Mifflin, 1964.

Mason, Ed. "Ike's First Fishing Hole." *Rod and Gun,* March 1955.

McDowell, Charles Jr. "Fred O. Seibel." *Richmond Times-Dispatch,* June 24, 1956.

McFeeley, William S. *Grant.* New York: W. W. Norton, 1981.

Merritt, Jim. "10th Angling President George Bush." *Fly Rod and Reel,* April 1989.

Mullins, Linda. *The Teddy Bear Men: Theodore Roosevelt and Clifford Berryman.* Cumberland: Hobby House, 1987.

Nash, Knowlton. *Kennedy & Diefenbaker.* Toronto: McClelland & Stewart, 1990.

Nevins, Allan. *Grover Cleveland: A Study in Courage.* New York: Dodd, Mead, 1932.

———, ed. *Letters of Grover Cleveland.* Boston: Houghton Mifflin, 1933.

Nixon, Richard. *In the Arena.* New York: Simon & Schuster, 1990.

O'Leary, John J. Jr. *Talks with T.R.* Boston: Houghton Mifflin, 1920.

Pictorial Biography of Harry S. Truman. New York: Grosset & Dunlop, 1975.

Raines, Howell. "In Fly Fishing, Carter's Record Can't Be Assailed." *New York Times,* May 4, 1991.

Ralph, Julian. "The President's Birthday" and others. *New York Sun,* September 28–October 8, 1883.

Randall, Ruth Painter. *Lincoln's Sons.* Boston: Little, Brown, 1955.

Reeves, Thomas. "President Arthur in Yellowstone National Park." *Montana, the Magazine of Western History,* Summer 1969, Vol. XIX, No. 3.

———. *Gentleman Boss.* New York: Knopf, 1975.

Reiger, John F. *American Sportsmen and the Origins of Conservation.* Norman, Okla.: University of Oklahoma Press, 1975.

Rigdon, William. *White House Sailor.* Garden City, N.Y.: Doubleday, 1962.

Rogers, Will. *How We Elect Our Presidents.* Boston: Little, Brown, 1952.

Roosevelt, Elliott. *As He Saw It.* New York: Duell, Sloan & Pearce, 1946.

Roosevelt, James. *Affectionately, F.D.R.* New York: Harcourt, Brace, 1959.

———. *My Parents: A Differing View.* Chicago: Playboy Press, 1976.

Roosevelt, Theodore. *Letters to His Children.* New York: Scribners, 1919.

———. *Theodore Roosevelt's Diaries of Boyhood and Youth.* New York: Charles Scribner's Sons, 1928.

———. *Letters of Theodore Roosevelt,* Vol. 6. Cambridge, Mass.: Harvard University Press, 1952.

———. *Through the Brazilian Wilderness.* New York: Charles Scribner's Sons, 1920.

———. "Harpooning Devilfish." *Scribner's,* Vol. LXII, No. 3, September 1917.

Sabato, Larry. *Feeding Frenzy.* New York: Free Press, 1991.

Schmitt, Waldo L. *The Presidential Cruise of 1938.* Washington: Smithsonian Institution, 1939.

Schullery, Paul. *American Fly Fishing: A History.* New York: Lyons & Burford, 1987.

———. "Theodore Roosevelt as an Angler." *The American Fly Fisher,* Summer 1982.

Shepley, James. "V.P.'s Fish Story." *Sports Illustrated,* April 25, 1955.

Smith, Merriman. *Meet Mister Eisenhower.* New York: Harper & Brothers, 1955.

Smith, Milford K. "Stray Shots and Short Casts." *Rutland Herald,* July 4, 1955.

Southard, Charles Z. *The Evolution of Trout and Trout Fishing in America.* New York: E. P. Dutton, 1928.

Starling, Edmund. As told to Thomas Sugrue. *Starling of the White House.* New York: Simon & Schuster, 1946.

Thompson, David S. *A Pictorial Biography: HST.* New York: Grosset & Dunlap, 1973.

Tourtellot, Arthur B. *The Presidents on the Presidency.* New York: Russell & Russell, 1964.

Troy, Gil. *See How They Ran.* Cambridge, Mass.: Harvard University Press, 1996.

Tully, Andrew. "Fishing With Ike." *Field & Stream,* September 1955.

Vest, G. G. "Notes of the Yellowstone Trip." *Forest and Stream,* Vol. XXI, November 8, 1882, p. 282.

Washington, George. *The Diaries of George Washington.* Donald Jackson and Dorothy Twohig, eds. Charlottesville, Va.: University Press of Virginia, 1976–1979.

——. *The Writings of George Washington.* John C. Fitzpatrick, ed. Washington: United States Government Printing Office, 1937.

Wechter, Dixon. *The Hero in America.* New York: Charles Scribner, 1941.

Weyandt, Dorothy. *I Was a Guide for Three U.S. Presidents.* Privately published, 1976.

Zern, Edward. *Hunting and Fishing from "A" to Zern.* New York: Lyons & Burford, 1985.

PERMISSIONS

Excerpts from *The Diaries of George Washington,* Donald Jackson and Dorothy Twohig eds. (Charlottesville: Virginia, 1976–79) reprinted with permission of the University Press of Virginia.

Print from *Sportman's Dictionary* reprinted courtesy of The Mount Vernon Ladies' Association.

Hand-drawn map of five farms at Mt. Vernon, Dec. 1793 reprinted by permission of *The Huntington Library.*

Illustration of Washington's account with a Jamaican firm used with permission of The Mount Vernon Ladies' Association.

Excerpt from *The Hero in America* by Dixon Wechter reprinted with the permission of Scribner, a Division of Simon & Schuster. Copyright 1941 by Charles Scribner's Sons; copyright renewed © 1969 by Elizabeth Farrar Wechter.

Excerpt from *Fishing for Fun* reprinted with permission of the Herbert Hoover Foundation and the Herbert Hoover Presidential Library Association, Inc.

Photographs of Eisenhower courtesy of the Eisenhower Presidential Library.

Excerpt from "George Bush" by Jim Merritt in *Rod & Reel* reprinted with permission of the *Outdoor Group.*

Photographs of Gerald R. Ford courtesy of the Gerald R. Ford Library.

Quote of President Carter from *An Outdoor Journal: Adventures and Reflections* reprinted with permission of the University of Arkansas Press.

Fred O. Seibel cartoons used with permission of the Special Collections Department, University of Virginia Library.

Excerpt from The Letters of Theodore Roosevelt, Vol. VI, edited by Elting E. Morison. Copyright © 1952 by the President and Fellows of Harvard College. Reprinted by permission of Harvard University Press.

Excerpts from Boilard interview used with permission of Robert A. Boilard.

Photographs of Presidents Grant and Arthur in the 1000 Islands used with permission of the Antique Boat Museum.

Photograph of Chester A. Arthur used with permission of the Library of Congress.

Clifford and Jim Berryman cartoons reprinted with permission of *The Washington Star.*

Photo of Calvin Coolidge inspecting the catch used with permission of J.R. Greene and the Calvin Coolidge Memorial Foundation.

Excerpt from *Starling of the White House* as told to Thomas Surrue by Colonel Edmund W. Starling reprinted with the permission of Simon & Schuster. Copyright © 1946, renewed 1973 by Simon & Schuster.

Cartoons by Karl Kae Knecht reprinted with permission of the *Evansville Courier.*

Photographs of Herbert Hoover courtesy of the Hoover Presidential Library.

Map by William Campbell courtesy of the Hoover Presidential Library.

Excerpt from *Homes of the Hoovers* by Ruth Dennis reprinted with permission of the Herbert Hoover Presidential Library.

Grover Page cartoon used with permission of the *Louisville Courier Journal.*

Cartoons by Darling courtesy of the J.N. "Ding" Darling Foundation.

Excerpts from *Affectionately, FDR* by James Roosevelt reprinted courtesy of Mrs. James Roosevelt.

Photos of President Carter fishing courtesy of the Jimmy Carter Library.

President Carter's remarks at groundbreaking originally appeared in *American Fly Fisherman.* Reprinted by permission of the Carter Center.

Photographs of President Bush used with permission of the Bush Presidential Library.

"Roosevelt's Fishing Vacation" by Vincent Svoboda used with permission of the Brooklyn Public Library Collection.

"Fishing Talk" by David Low reprinted with permission of *Evening Standard/Solo.*

Photograph by Aldo Merusi used with permission of the *Rutland Herald*.

Excerpt from "Stray Shots and Short Casts" by Milford K. Smith reprinted with permission of the *Rutland Herald*.

Excerpt from *Philosophical Fisherman* reprinted with permission of the Lyons Press. Copyright © 1969 by Harold Blaisdell.

Photograph of President Harding and wife from the Robert Runyon Photographic Collection used with permission of the Center for American History, the University of Texas at Austin.

Letter to Dr. Curtis W. Garrison from Fanny Hayes used with permission of the Rutherford B. Hayes Presidential Center.

Excerpt from interview with Wayne Harpster used with permission.

Quote of Professor George Harvey used with permission.

Excerpt from interview with Rosalynn Carter used with permission.

Photograph of Herbert Hoover used with permission of the American Museum of Fly Fishing.

Photograph of Jimmy Carter and Vince Marinaro used with permission of the American Museum of Fly Fishing.

Excerpt from an article by Howell Raines. Copyright © 1991 by the New York Times Company. Reprinted by permission.

Cartoon by Norm Muffit reprinted courtesy of *Deh Cho Drum* Northern News Services Limited.

Photograph of Grover Cleveland from the Woodrow Wilson Collection used with permission of the Princeton University Library.

INDEX

Illustrations indicated by page numbers in italics.

Bill Mares, a *cum laude* graduate in history from Harvard, is the author of eight previous books and a former member of the Vermont House of Representatives. He has contributed freelance pieces to the *Christian Science Monitor* and the *Economist*. He teaches history at Champlain Valley Union High School in Vermont.